WORKING
AND
LIKING IT

Also by Richard Germann and Peter Arnold:
JOB AND CAREER BUILDING

WORKING
AND
LIKING IT

RICHARD GERMANN
DIANE BLUMENSON
AND
PETER ARNOLD

FAWCETT COLUMBINE / NEW YORK

A Fawcett Columbine Book
Published by Ballantine Books
Copyright © 1984 by Richard Germann,
Diane Blumenson, and Peter Arnold

Library of Congress Catalog Card Number: 83-91174
ISBN 0-449-90084-3

Manufactured in the United States of America
First Edition: April 1984

10 9 8 7 6 5 4 3 2 1

TO ELI DJEDDAH   1911–1981
Our Source of Inspiration

CONTENTS

ACKNOWLEDGMENTS

The authors are pleased to acknowledge with gratitude the contributions, both direct and indirect, of a large number of people. It is not possible to name all of them here, but they will recognize their contributions in the many examples given throughout this book.

We want to mention specifically the three persons who left the greatest imprint on this book: the late Eli Djeddah, on whose human relations concepts much of the book is based; Bernard Haldane, who first brought practical career counseling out of the dark ages and gave it life; and the work and writings of Richard Bolles, another, more indirect source of inspiration to the authors.

The direct contributions of Sally Everson Bates, Eleanor Bushman, Gary Cardone, Marjorie Cram, David Estridge, Ann Hathaway, Dick Hill, Joe Puffer, and Paul Stanger are acknowledged with gratitude.

Also, thanks to Lowell Martin, Natalie Dawes and Linda Gerber for their support and assistance. Sheridan Germann, Paul Cook, and Margery Arnold provided both moral support and tangible contributions.

Special thanks go to Gail Norcross, whose intelligence made sense out of handwritten notes, and who produced the final typed manuscript of the book.

Finally, the authors wish to thank Felicia Eth, Joelle Delbourgo, and Alice Fahs for making the publication of this material possible.

INTRODUCTION

Do you like your job? If you're like most people, you like at least *part* of your job. Few people stumble into a job entirely by accident. There's usually *something* about a job that's right. And a lot of things that could be improved, if you knew how.

Again, if you're like most people you believe that it is reasonable to expect satisfaction and a chance to use your greatest talents and skills in your work. What you may not have realized clearly is that landing the right job by no means guarantees you job satisfaction for more than a few days. Where do you go from there?

Picture yourself driving your car in a lovely part of the country, miles from anywhere. For no clearly visible reason, the engine sputters, coughs, and comes to a complete halt. You're now stuck with a beautiful view from horizon to horizon. The view does not contain a service station or another vehicle.

You have three choices: You can get out and kick the tires; you can sit down by the side of the road and cry; or you can get out your tool kit, open the hood, and fix the car. You don't know how? Too bad.

Many people now realize that a course in basic automobile mechanics is a good idea. But few believe that it requires any skill to fix a *job* that has sputtered and come to a halt, or just needs some basic maintenance. This explains why it has been estimated that four out of five people are not happy in their jobs.

Working and Liking It is, in a sense, an owner's manual for your job. Any job. After reading this book, you'll be able to repair and rebuild your job. You'll also be able to transform it into a much better one and to maintain it at that level.

The approach and principles described may sound too good to be true, but they are derived entirely from what *works.* We have excluded any theories that have not produced results, however much they may have been accepted by many as truths in the work world.

For the methodology to be converted into results, activity is required. And a certain amount of patience. Taking shortcuts will render many of the practices described in this book ineffective. However—and this is the core of our approach—the actions required are positive, the results are rewarding, and the fringe benefits are visible almost from the very beginning.

WORKING
AND
LIKING IT

CHAPTER 1

WORKING
AND
LIKING IT

How do you feel about going to work tomorrow morning? We recently asked a friend this question and got a depressing answer. He said: "I can hardly make myself go into the office. If I didn't have a family to support, I wouldn't work at all."

Being professional busybodies, we couldn't leave his answer alone: "If you feel this way, why don't you do something about it?" we asked. "Oh—I've been looking around, but jobs at my level are hard to find." Undaunted—we've heard that so often before—we switched tactics: "Your company is one of the most prestigious in your field. Surely there must be opportunities within the organization for someone with your ability."

His somewhat violent, but to us predictable response was: "Are you insane? I've told you about my boss. Can you imagine what he'd do to me if I told him how I felt about my job? I'd be out on the street within

1

minutes. No—I'll just keep doing my job the best way I can, and look forward to weekends when I can do what I like. After all, work isn't everything."

We don't know about work being everything, but we do know that working and *not* liking it is a terrible waste of the gift of life. Having helped many people find their way to liking their work, and even sometimes loving it, we decided to write a book to help our friend and others in similar traps.

Before we go more deeply into the subject of liking your work, there is one ground rule to keep in mind.

Liking Your Work Is Essential For Your Success, However You Define Success. If You Don't Enjoy Your Work, You Will Ultimately Fail.

This may seem like an extreme statement. If you think so, you may agree with people who believe "you don't have to love your work to succeed—you just have to be good at it."

Just being good at your work without really getting day-to-day enjoyment from doing it may provide some success in the short-term. It *never* results in success in the long run.

The case of a young electronics engineer provides one example. Within an eight-year period, he had made five job changes, increasing his salary each time. When asked why he moved so frequently, he replied, "I'd simply get bored with the work and the company, and I always knew when to leave before making too many enemies." His crisis point came when it became harder for him to find alternative employment, and all of his relationships in his job, as well as his professional reputation, began to deteriorate.

This is neither an extreme nor uncommon example. Not liking one's work is the cause for most career changes, as well as for a large percentage of firings and layoffs.

This example also reveals what a crucial factor people are in liking your work. Your job environment isn't just furniture, space, rules, systems, and procedures: It's made up of people as well. How you feel about your physical environment and the rules and systems affecting your job depends in large part on how you feel about your people environment.

When you feel good about and are in control of your people environment, you are automatically in control of *all* other parts of your job environment.

In this book you'll not only learn how to manage your people environment, but also how to systematically transform your job from something you just do to something you truly enjoy doing. Every day of the week.

Before we can get started on this subject, there are two things *you* must do. First, make sure that the job you have is one you believe is worth doing from your point of view. Second, open your mind to new, nontraditional thinking about your job environment and your power to influence and change it.

Traditional thinking has led to a number of myths that have had a destructive effect on people's thinking about job satisfaction, career advancement, and their job environment. In the next few pages we'll show you each of these myths, followed by an updated view of reality. This updated view will broaden your perspective on working and interacting in your job (people) environment.

Myth: Happiness is a management position.
Reality: Happiness for many people is being released from the national mania of seeking a management position as the one and only true measure of success. Management is a specialized skill, just as

basket weaving, systems analysis, and selling are specialized skills. For the skilled manager, it is the highest form of achievement. For the wrong person, it is a source of misery and nervous exhaustion. This conclusion is reinforced by the huge number of unhappy and ineffective people currently trapped in management positions.

Myth: Greater responsibility is accompanied by greater aggravation.

Reality: If your area of responsibility coincides with your greatest skill, talent, and motivation, there is almost no limit to the energy you can bring to your work, and aggravation is spelled *challenge*.

Myth: Advancement means promotion from one job to a different one.

Reality: Advancement usually adds to, rather than changes, your responsibilities. For example, if you are a successful salesperson, it doesn't necessarily follow that you'll be an effective sales manager. But if you are a good sales manager in a local office, you may well be an effective regional or national sales manager.

Dr. Laurence J. Peter developed the "Peter Principle" from his observation that promotion from a job well done to a higher-level job may lead to "occupational incompetence." On this reasonable observation, however, he built what we believe to be an extreme and potentially dangerous theory: "In a hierarchy every employee tends to rise to his level of incompetence." Extreme—because it's a sweeping generalization. And potentially dangerous—because it implies that you and I have little or no control over our job and career destinies. From our experience and research, we know that this is untrue.

The tools we'll provide you with in this book will enable you to advance meaningfully and effectively.

Myth: My job description dictates my job.
Reality: A job description is a plan, subject to change as reality demands.

In fact, most job descriptions change imperceptibly, almost on a daily basis. If you want proof, write an accurate description of your current daily activities and compare it with your original job description. Better yet, ask your boss how he or she sees your job, then compare that version with the one you prepared. You'll almost certainly find major discrepancies.

This is as it should be. Once a job description has become a straitjacket, it no longer serves a useful purpose. We'll show you how to adapt your job and your job description to reality, to the company's goals, and to your own goals.

Myth: The only way I can move up is for my boss to retire or die.
Reality: There are many ways to advance, short of leaving the company. To list a few:
- Help your boss to advance
- Take the initiative in assisting your company to develop a new business area
- Transfer to another department where the chances of advancement are better.

But be sure to ask yourself: Is promotion the only way for me to grow? And see the above discussion of seeking management positions.

Myth: In order to become more valuable/promotable, I should take courses in my areas of weakness.

Reality: Take courses in your areas of strength. Become the best there is in those areas.

Learning to overcome areas of weakness is time consuming, often distasteful, and usually results in being "better at" but not "great at" whatever the weakness. Being mediocre at something never increases your value to your employer.

On the other hand, being the best there is in areas you enjoy and in which you can perform energetically will always add to your value in the work world.

Myth: The company/policy/personnel department/boss decides when I get a raise and how much it will be.

Reality: You can take control of your own advancement, including the timing and size of salary increases, by using the techniques described in this book.

Myth: The squeaky wheel gets the grease.

Reality: The "working" squeaky wheel gets the grease. If you are productive, and let people know that you are, you will get the attention you deserve.

Myth: Don't make waves.

Reality: Make constructive waves only. Examples of destructive wavemakers are:
  • Chronic complainers and critics
  • On-the-job empire builders

- Speeders—people who get ahead of everyone else, thereby upsetting the natural rhythm of their organization.

The common denominator of all compulsive wavemakers is that they are out of tune with the organizations in which they work. Examples of *constructive* wavemaking are:

- Demonstrating enthusiasm for the organization and its goals
- Creating excitement in others about the purpose of the organization, leading to better teamwork and higher productivity.

Myth: Company policy determines everything about my job.

Reality: Company policy is necessary to give directions to an organization, to set goals, to help achieve them, and to prevent chaos. But it is as flexible and changeable as the people who make it. We will show you how you can constructively influence your company's policy.

Myth: If I don't get a raise, that's a personal rejection.

Reality: Not necessarily; not even very often. Unfortunately, most people make the immediate assumption that a raise withheld is a direct reflection on their job performance.

When asked, "If you request a raise and don't get it, what should you do? Too many people answer: "Start looking for another job."

The first thing to do when your boss says you won't get a raise is quite simple. Ask for an explanation. You can usually find out what caused the omission and take positive action. We'll show you how.

> *Myth:* When a woman or member of a minority group is denied advancement, it's obviously prejudice at work.
>
> *Reality:* It may or may not be. Don't make an assumption. There are ways of finding out without destructive confrontation.

Assuming that denial of advancement is based on prejudice is in itself a discriminatory practice. The ability to communicate effectively, both to give information and to *get* information, is essential to your ability to discover the actual reasons for the decisions made by your superiors. We'll show you how to communicate constructively so that your actions can be based on the circumstances. Taking any action without full knowledge of what really occurred can severely damage your job and career growth.

> *Myth:* No woman has ever held such a position in this organization, so it's impossible for me to get it.
>
> *Reality:* Precedent doesn't necessarily dictate policy, nor does it necessarily indicate deep prejudice. There's a first time for everything, especially if you can show that it is in the company's best interest.

We've all observed significant advancement for women in one industry after another. You may be employed in one of the die-hard, male chauvinist industries, but you can be certain that in the industries where women no longer have such barriers, one woman broke through them first.

In most cases, she did it by providing evidence that her advancement would directly benefit the organization.

Myth: The best way to get ahead is to "butter up" your boss.

Reality: Insincerity may get short-range results, but it's a sure way to long-run oblivion. Few bosses are either unaware of or welcome such tactics, especially on major issues. It pays, however, to develop a tactful way to communicate with your boss (and everyone else) when you disagree. Responding to your boss with "I think you're dead wrong" is equally as unsuccessful as "Anything you say, J.B."

Replace tactlessness and insincerity with solutions to honest disagreements. For instance, "I understand your concern. I have some ideas about this I'd like to discuss with you."

Myth: "My boss is the only person who can help me grow in the company. He is my mentor. If he leaves, I'll be out of luck."

Reality: This is rarely true, but this myth does reveal the need to communicate with others in the organization. Having a boss who is personally interested in your job growth and development is certainly advantageous. Relying on your boss as the single source for your motivation and knowledge, however, is tantamount to relinquishing control of your future.

Myth: The only thing management cares about is profit.

Reality: There is no such thing as "management." There are only people. To see management as a monolithic unit is to cut yourself off from any possibility of communicating with the very people who control your work environment and, therefore, have power over a sizable segment of your life.

Every management group has a list of priorities that is constantly shifting. Each person within that group also has his or her own priorities. In a profit-making organization, it is reasonable to place profits high on the list of priorities because without profits, there would be no company and no job. But it is a gross oversimplification to assume that no other motivation exists.

In fact one of the most constructive and exciting things you can do in your job is to find out what your superiors' goals and purposes are and what motivates your employers individually and collectively. If you can understand and genuinely relate to their goals and purposes, a large part of your job satisfaction and future is assured.

Myth: In times of economic recession, it's best to do your work quietly and stop thinking about advancement.

Reality: Wrong! In periods of economic downturn, organizations really *need* ideas for greater efficiency, savings, and productivity—and, sometimes, survival. There are many opportunities for people with ideas.

Myth: My problem is unique. No one can possibly understand it unless that person
has been in the exact same situation.

Reality: It may seem that way, but problems are
subject to analysis and are reducible, in
part, to common factors or principles.
Once the principles are recognized, solutions can be found.

Institutions, corporations, the public sector, the private sector, engineering, academia, law, medicine, advertising, publishing, the arts, communications—all
have vastly different components and a wide variety of
structures. Yet there is one thing all organizations and
career fields have in common: They are made up of
people.

In the work world, people who interact with each
other tend to act in surprisingly similar ways, wherever they work and whatever jobs they perform. So basic
human relations skills can be applied in virtually any
work situation to achieve a positive response.

Myth: It isn't necessary to advance in a job in
order to be happy.

Reality: No organization can remain static. In
order to survive, it must grow and
change with its environment. The same
is true of every individual within an organization.

Although you can grow in your job without being promoted, the real meaning of advancement is to get better at what you do, to grow in knowledge, skill, and
maturity.

An important factor to consider in judging the accuracy of many of the statements people make about the work place is the motivation of those making the statements. If you say that company policy prevents you from taking any action in a certain area, you may really be saying: "It's more trouble than it's worth for me to take the action." This then becomes a subjective decision. Everyone has a right to make such decisions, but once this subjective judgment is packaged as seemingly objective advice given to others, it becomes a destructive force and a cause of major job unhappiness.

Having cleared away the underbrush of myth and misconception, you are now ready to turn to the subject of job satisfaction, and what it means to you.

CHAPTER 2

DEFINING JOB SATISFACTION FOR YOU

The responsibility for liking your job and creating the conditions for job satisfaction is yours. Although you can enlist your employer's cooperation, your job satisfaction never becomes your employer's responsibility. That isn't to say that disliking your work is your *fault*. Doing something about it is your responsibility simply because no one else can do it.

If you expect your boss to take the initiative on your behalf, you'll probably find yourself at a dead end, as the following example illustrates:

George M. worked as a personnel manager for a manufacturing company. Looking for a way to make his job more exciting and perhaps add to his responsibilities, he inquired of his boss, "What can I do to make my job less monotonous? I'd like a chance to grow." His boss's reaction was, "We need you where you are; you're doing a good job. What exactly did you have in mind?"

George's response—"I don't know"— left them at an impasse.

After some thought and counseling, George decided to take a different approach:

"I feel I could benefit the company by expanding the personnel department to go beyond its present function of wage and salary administration. I'd like to create a training and development program to educate employees about the purpose of the company and its products. The kind of program I have in mind would also help our employees develop to their fullest capacity, and eventually reduce employee turnover."

With this initiative George took the onus off his boss to come up with ideas for his job growth. Few bosses have the time or inclination to solve your career problems.

Job satisfaction is part of a work-life continuum. Building a wall between your work and the other parts of your life, (avocation, leisure, continuing education) is self-defeating. Expending all of your energy on your job, at the expense of other things in life, is just as unproductive as seeing your job only as a means of producing income to be spent on the better things. Often the better things turn sour, and the income won't come in for very long.

Jason K., for example, believed he could best pursue his career as an Abstract Expressionist painter by making the ample wages of a construction worker. In doing so, he felt he would provide himself with the ability to live comfortably, purchase the necessary supplies for his artistic career, and enable himself to appear not as a starving artist but as a successful, well-fed entrepreneur. Several of his friends had tried this approach.

It didn't take very long for his plan to backfire on every level. First of all, he was so exhausted from the construction job that he could rarely paint. Second, he was socially out of tune with the other workers and felt he was severely disliked. Finally, when there was a minor cutback of personnel, his boss felt Jason should be the first to go, since he didn't really like the work or the people he worked with.

An astute career counselor once stated: "It's almost impossible *not* to use your greatest skills and talents; in fact, it's probably harder than not eating."

For this reason, people gravitate towards avocations and leisure activities where they can happily employ capabilities which are not being used in their jobs.

But when the skills and talents you like to use are too heavily loaded into leisure or avocational activities, and your employment becomes a tedious means to support those activities, the system backfires.

"I found myself moving through my work day like a robot," said a manufacturing manager who loved to coach sports activities after hours. "The only excitement I had was the anticipation of getting through with work so I could be with the kids. But after a while I found that I was so depressed and tired that I couldn't even enjoy coaching."

Before we continue using the phrase "job satisfaction," let's define it. There are probably as many definitions as there are definers. Here are some typical ones:

"Job satisfaction is being able to make my own decisions."

"For me, it's being recognized for a job well done."

"Marketing is what I love to do. Taking an unknown product and making it a household word is really satisfying to me."

"I have to make what I consider a good amount of money to feel satisfied in my work."

"If I can't work out-of-doors, I'm never satisfied. That's essential for me."

"Working with young children is a necessary part of work for me."

"I'm very satisfied if people respect me for my professionalism and integrity. Money is not my top priority."

"I really enjoy the academic setting. I think I need it to be truly happy in my work."

"Risk taking is very exciting to me. I'm addicted to making decisions that could make or break a company."

"Investment counseling is all the job satisfaction I need. It's not like work to me. It's like gambling, winning, and getting paid for it."

There is a common denominator in all of these definitions: *Job satisfaction increases when the job fits your unique personality, both in terms of your life values and the maximum use of your greatest talents and abilities.*

During a television interview, actor Tony Randall said that he never could really understand how people were willing to pay him for what he loves to do. He said he'd be willing to pay *them* to let him do it.

One of the drawbacks of thinking of your work as simply a means of support is that you are tempted to draw a firm line between work and leisure. Between what produces income and what doesn't. Between what your employer tells you to do and what you tell yourself to do.

This line can be a major barrier to work enjoyment. It may, on closer examination, turn out to be entirely artificial.

You can prove this to yourself by doing the following exercise: On a piece of paper, write down the functions or activities you carry out during a typical day or other convenient time period. Then decide which of these activities are so natural to you that you also engage in them away from your job, albeit in a different form. Your list may look something like this:

OWNER OF SMALL COMPANY

ON-THE-JOB FUNCTIONS	OFF-THE-JOB ACTIVITIES
Budgeting	Budgeting for travel; household treasurer for Model Railroad Association
Conducting meetings	Presiding over Tenants Association meetings; leading church fund drive
Writing reports	None
Designing office environments	Designed addition on house; redesigned kitchen
Purchasing and price negotiations	Buying antiques for collection

EXECUTIVE SECRETARY

ON-THE-JOB FUNCTIONS	OFF-THE-JOB ACTIVITIES
Typing	Typing manuscripts for friends
Making travel arrangements	None
Setting up staff meetings	Chairwoman for genealogical society; setting up meetings and social gatherings
Filing	Developed genealogical system

Handling written and oral communications	Frequent written and telephone communications with members of genealogical society
Decision making	Making all family financial decisions

Having illustrated that you use many of your skills and talents in all areas of your life, on and off the job, the obvious next step is to determine what it is that makes you happy in your work—what the major factors are that produce job fulfillment for you.

It stands to reason that you're not going to be absolutely in love with each and every task and function you will perform in your job. But it's essential to your work enjoyment that you do more of the things you really enjoy than things you don't like doing. In fact, the object is to move toward 100 percent of the likes and 0 percent of the dislikes, even though you may never reach the ideal.

Roland M., for example, was vice-president of marketing for a national investment counseling firm. The role he preferred was developing new investment packages and training sales personnel. But most of his work—perhaps 60 percent—was devoted to policing his staff and keeping up with paperwork. He found that boring. So, over a period of time, Roland was able to delegate a large portion of paperwork and most of the routine supervisory duties to other members of his staff, while retaining overall control. This brought him closer to his goal of 100 percent likable tasks and 0 percent of the ones he disliked.

Some people equate job satisfaction with continual movement up the organizational ladder of responsibility and power. For these people it is obviously important to find a way to constantly increase the value of their work to their employer while simultaneously seeking to increase the number of functions they enjoy and do well.

> Amanda D., for example, was an account executive at a growing public relations firm. She loved designing the promotional packages, acting as liaison between the client and the public relations firm, and managing media events. On the other hand, she tired easily of writing press releases and generally got bored with research projects.
>
> Determined to move up the ladder quickly, while ridding herself of her most distasteful tasks, Amanda concentrated her efforts on bringing in as much new business as possible. In doing so, she was able to justify hiring writers to take over the functions she disliked. Eventually she brought in so much business that she was promoted to vice-president.

But what if you say: "I have no interest in getting ahead. The rat race is not for me—I just want to do a good job and be left alone?" The short answer is that every organization desparately needs people who are good at what they do and who perform their work reliably day after day, year after year. (Note that "reliably" is not the same as "unthinkingly" or robotlike.)

A more complete answer is that there is no such thing as standing still in the world of work. Nothing in life stands still. Every organization is in a constant state of movement; it expands or contracts, changes, grows, or recedes. This also applies to the human dynamics within the organization. So even the person who quietly does his job day in and day out must be aware of and move with the employer's purposes—or become an unhappy misfit. The case of a market research assistant illustrates this point well:

> "For many years, I've successfully collected quality data and compiled information that I know will result

in really good reports. My boss always comments on how accurate my information is, but recently he has stopped using my reports in his final presentations. I really like what I do, but I don't get any recognition anymore. My boss hasn't said so, but I'm afraid he's thinking of getting rid of me."

It is apparent that this market research assistant continues to provide the same kind of reports that were both relevant and valuable to the boss in the past. Times change, and not knowing what is relevant and valuable to the boss today has left this man frustrated, dissatisfied, and in fear of losing his job. Another example of being conservative to the point of inflexibility is the case of David G.

David had been chief engineer for an optical equipment firm for eight years. The company he worked for was about to bid on a large contract to manufacture a new type of scanning device. The contract would put the company into a new line of business and bring in millions of dollars in profits.

Designing the equipment for a presentation to the industrial user of the new scanner would have to be done at great speed. In fact, a working prototype was needed in four months. Normally, it would take a full year.

Despite the rush, David insisted that the firm's traditional standards be upheld and methods followed, even if that meant losing the contract. To his dismay, upper management took the job out of David's hands, hiring extra technicians and a top level engineer to head the project. The company won the contract.

David believed that his previous level of high standards was all he needed to maintain in order to function securely as chief engineer. Unfortunately, he was unable to respond to changing needs and lost a major portion of his responsibilities, thereby actually moving backwards in the company.

What does your ideal job look like?

For an hour or so, let yourself go. Write down your personal vision of job utopia. We'll get to *realistic* goal setting in the next chapter. For now allow yourself to dream. Without *ideal* goals there would be no *realistic* goals. Any realism that doesn't incorporate idealism isn't worth striving for.

For the purpose of this exercise, don't worry where, indeed if, there is such a job. Break your ideal job down into these categories:

- Your ideal job functions or activities (what you enjoy doing)
- Your authority and reporting level (from complete independence all the way to chief executive officer or chairman of the board)
- The type of company or organization you'd like to be associated with
- The type of people you'd like to be surrounded by on the job
- The ideal physical space (large window office, out-doors, etc.)
- The kind and amount of income you'd like to have (commission, salary, bonus, etc.)
- Where you'd like to be five years from now.

If you find this a depressing activity, you're not dreaming enough! If it's *fun*, you're on the right track. When you've finished this exercise, repeat it with a different set of duties and circumstances. Most people find there is more than one setting for their ideal job. Whatever you do, don't lose any of these pieces of paper. Keep them handy for ideas when you're ready to set realistic goals for yourself.

This kind of exercise is a very personal matter. But

ve've been given permission to publish the following deal job descriptions (job utopias):

Joseph C.:

My ideal job is to be a travel guide in Greece, using my extensive knowledge of ancient Greece. This would be my own business. I would make all travel arrangements for groups of ten to twenty people, including trips to historical, artistic, archeological, and resort locations.

I would like to guide individuals who have a sincere interest in the history of the countries they visit and who generally have gourmet tastes.

My ideal tour would take me to all parts of the country at a leisurely pace, with time to seriously experience the history and art, as well as to enjoy the beautiful resorts.

The income I would earn for operating these tours would cover my own expenses and enable me to net approximately $15,000 for the year.

In just five years, I'd like to be running a tour company, where I would design trips to all parts of Europe, manage three to five guides, and act as guide on a maximum of three trips per year. My net income should be at least $40,000.

Eva T.

My ideal job would be office manager in a large law firm where I could use my personnel management, administrative, and human relations skills. I would be completely responsible for all clerical, secretarial, and paralegal employees. I would report directly to the senior partners.

The people I'd be working with on a day-to-day basis would all be well-trained professionals and would contribute to an orderly, businesslike daily environment.

The office space I see myself in would have an open feeling, with basic contemporary lines and lots of windows.

My income would be $35,000 or more.

In five years, I'd like to be the head of a national paralegal personnel agency, with an income of $75,000.

Before we can go on to talk about realistic goal setting, we need to state a guiding principle for all job and work goals. We've hinted at it before: *The world of work is a world of people.* Virtually every aspect of your job is shaped and controlled by the people involved and their relationships with each other.

Since people, and your relationships with them, are a vital aspect of your job, and therefore of any plan to improve or change it, no job goal can be realistic unless it takes interpersonal relationships into account.

With this keen awareness of the importance of people in your job environment, you are now ready to start setting some realistic goals to get you on the way to your own personal vision of job and career fulfillment.

CHAPTER 3

REALISTIC GOAL SETTING

In chapter 2 we defined job satisfaction. The next step is to express your own definition of job satisfaction in terms of realistic job and work goals.

You probably know a few people who are genuinely inspired by the work they do and a lot who aren't. All of us tend to jump to the conclusion that *what is, must be.* We keep hearing from those around us, including our national leaders, that unpleasant facts are a reality of life and must be accepted as such.

We are told there are no "quick fixes" to problems, and that nonacceptance of these problems as more or less permanent facts of life amounts to unrealistic idealism. Yet most great advances in civilization have been brought about by people who have refused to accept the status quo as a permanent condition.

For most of us, bringing about changes in international relations or the national economy is not a realistic objective. We aren't trained for it. But changing our daily work environment is, by comparison, an easy objective to achieve. For many of the people interviewed for this book, changing their work and their work environment was only the first step. Some have gone on to use the tools and experience they developed in this process to teach and help others gain job satisfaction.

We will be making frequent use of the words "goal" and "objective" in this chapter. By goal we mean a long-range purpose to be achieved, while the word objective denotes a *specific, next-step* plan to achieve that goal.

Let's start on our discussion of goal and objective setting with an example:

Howard G. began work in the engineering department of a manufacturing firm as product development specialist. After six months in this position, it was clear to him that he wasn't using his greatest talents, which were more people oriented than thing oriented. Analysis of his achievements in his life up to that point showed that he was at his best when he used his considerable persuasive and sales abilities in product development. He didn't have much opportunity to use these skills and found himself stagnating.

He studied the way the company was organized and talked to a number of people to scout for needs in other departments where he might apply his sales skill to relevant company needs. When it became clear to him that sales training was a neglected function in the organization, he set out to make a job change within the company. His *long-range goal* was a senior management position.

Howard's *first objective* was to transfer to the marketing department. By clearly identifying a need, and by providing a reasonable proposal with proof of his product knowledge, loyalty to the company, and sales ability, Howard got support to make the transition.

In this new position, Howard moved from salesman to sales trainer to upper management. Throughout his career growth, Howard applied his knowledge of skills analysis to help the men and women in the sales force identify their own best capabilities. In a few instances, this resulted in members of the sales group relocating to other departments for greater effectiveness. Howard showed these people how to develop and use the resources available to them for locating the most suitable positions for themselves.

The result of Howard's approach was a highly successful sales team composed only of people who were using their greatest skills and found their greatest rewards in sales and marketing.

In this chapter we will show you the wealth of choices available to you. We hope to inspire you to think big, to convince you that there is hardly anything in your job and in your work environment that you can't influence and improve, provided you take one step at a time and follow the ground rules laid out in this book.

Let's take a look now at specific objectives to help you expand your thinking. In reality the range of possible objectives is virtually infinite. But they tend to fall into categories:

TAKING ON ADDED RESPONSIBILITIES

There are a number of ways to do this. A task may fall into your area of expertise or talent but may be drudgery to the person currently responsible for it.

Jane's strengths included written communications and verbal skills. What's more, she was highly motivated to use these skills, but as research assistant to the marketing director of a national food distributor, there seemed little opportunity to do so. One possibility that she'd been eyeing was to write the employee newsletter. The publication was read faithfully by over two hundred employees, but was being written with little enthusiasm or professionalism by the marketing director's secretary. By relieving the secretary of what she felt was a boring and thankless job and adding this task to her own list of responsibilities, Jane provided herself with a chance to prove her skill in a new area and, as a fringe benefit, earned the undying gratitude of the marketing department secretary.

Another way to take on extra responsibilities, when you have spare time and energy, is to lift one or two duties off your boss's shoulders and onto your own. In addition, every organization has things that need to be done but don't exactly fall into any one person's defined area of responsibility.

PROMOTION TO A HIGHER LEVEL

It's your responsibility to make sure that you don't move, or get moved, into an area or a level which is out of tune with your greatest skills, no matter how prestigious or well paid. This is an example of the Peter Principle, or being promoted to your level of incompetence. But it's easy to avoid: The more promotable you are, the more leverage and control you have over the new responsibility you take on. Let's return once again to Howard G.'s case:

You'll recall that sales and training were among his greatest talents. Imagine a hypothetical development: Howard does his job and waits for recognition and a promotion for being a great sales trainer. His boss sends a memo:

"You've proven your skill and competence at sales training as well as your superior knowledge of our product. We'd like you to be our new director of market research." The memo is very flattering, but Howard hates research!

Now we'll alter the scenario and let Howard take part in the process. Instead of waiting for his boss to make the first move, he makes his own proposal for a senior sales management position as well as a new incentive plan for sales commissions and a program for increasing the company's sales territory.

A LATERAL MOVE

Often you find that the fit between work being done in another department or area of the company and your own preferences and skills is much better than the fit in your current job. We will introduce here a very useful device called the Contact/Information Network, or the C/I Network for short, which will be described in greater detail in chapter 4. The C/I Network is a group of people in your organization with whom you have an easy talking relationship and from whom you can get reliable, off-the-record information about events, decisions, and just about anything you may need to know in order to plan your next move.

In the case of a lateral move, you may need to recruit one or two new C/I Network members who know about the area you are interested in. The ubiquitous Howard G. is an example of this kind of move.

From assistant-to-the-president to sales trainer, Howard's objective was not to move up, but over—into an area where he could use his best abilities. In order to make his move, he involved his C/I Network to learn about the company's sales department, how it operated, and how he might fit in. The information he got enabled him to set a realistic objective that was within the structure of the organization and a response to a confirmed need.

A SALARY INCREASE

You may wonder how the preliminary steps described earlier in this and other chapters are relevant to receiving a simple increase in salary. The answer is that beyond an automatic cost-of-living raise, every increase is related to other parts of your job and your job performance. Substantial increases are justified in any one or all of the other categories mentioned above and below. The most desirable salary increase is the one where your entire job is redefined at a different, and higher, level, and a new compensation arrangement is negotiated.

> Marilyn A. is an example of this approach. Her job as assistant to the director of data processing for a national market research firm included responsibility for the administration of the firm's innovative data maintenance system. Her goal was to redefine her job—to become director of data maintenance and negotiate a large salary increase on the basis of her new status.

PARTICIPATION IN THE BUSINESS ORGANIZATION

Provided your contributions in the past warrant it, participation such as stock in the company or partnership status are often realistic objectives. One of the most important factors with this type of objective is your loyalty to your company, real and perceived. Much of that depends on your positive relationship with others.

> A classic example of this is the goal to become a partner in a law firm. Hugh C. discovered the importance

of his relationships with the senior members of his firm in his quest to become a partner. He believed he was passed over for consideration at one point because of tension in his relationship with two of the more venerable partners.

Through his C/I Network, he discovered that a number of partners felt he was simply not interested in the success of the firm as a business. They also felt that Hugh's disinterest in the various social functions of the firm indicated to some that he was not a particularly loyal worker.

With this information in hand, Hugh set out to develop positive relationships with three of the most influential partners. He communicated regularly on the more important aspects of his cases and made it a point to show his genuine concern for the welfare of the firm. As Hugh finally developed the image of a loyal and dedicated member of the organization, he was made a partner.

A NEW TITLE OR A NEW JOB DESCRIPTION

These are relatively easy to negotiate, as long as they are substantiated (see chapter 8). Usually a new title is *followed* by a corresponding increase in compensation. The rule of thumb here is: Don't ask for a title or a new job description *and* money at the same time. Allow people to get used to your new title and the status that goes with it. Justify the new job description by doing the work. *Then* ask for the corresponding salary increase. It will be seen as your due and will be easy to get. For example:

Paul C. automatically took on responsibility for managing the traffic department of a large import firm when his boss abruptly resigned. After a month of doing the job, he proposed that his title be changed from "Traffic Coordinator" to "Traffic Manager." He had no trouble getting approval.

Another month passed. Paul felt he had made the transition to his new status and was accepted by the other members of the company as a manager. He proposed a salary increase to correspond with his job level and received it without argument.

A new job description may, in fact, represent a career change for you.

This was the case with Ellen B. Her goal was to move from a position as director of labor and delivery nurses to head nurse for the entire hospital. In her new function, she no longer performed any nursing tasks but was using administrative and management skills to direct a staff of more than one hundred people.

UNLOADING OR DELEGATING UNWANTED DUTIES

This is something few people ever think of. You don't have to live with duties that you find distasteful. Your C/I Network will often help you to identify people who love to do the things that drive you up the wall.

Marvin G., for example, found that his job as director of engineering for a growing electronics firm was becoming more a policing function than an engineering one. As the organization grew and more engineers were hired, the administration of the increasing number of projects being done, as well as daily operations supervision, made it impossible for him to be involved in the engineering design process. He solved his problem by assigning the operations function to an engineer whose main interest was company management.

Delegation of duties isn't restricted to delegating down. You can occasionally delegate to people at your level—but only with their consent, of course. Beware of delegating upwards. When you find yourself unloading tasks on your boss, you may be courting swift retribution.

You can often combine the taking on of new duties and the delegating of unwanted ones in a trade-off with the right person.

A CHANGE IN YOUR PHYSICAL ENVIRONMENT

This may be a move from one office to another, or a move to another part of the country. It may be a move from outdoor work to indoor work or vice versa.

Robert J. was the manager of operations of a national food franchise. Most of his time was spent at his desk in a small office. He was starting to hate his job and looked for ways to escape his office, not realizing at first that his problem was simply the amount of time he had to spend within its four walls.

An accidental conversation with one of the firm's founders unearthed the fact that before Robert joined the firm, his department was responsible for the inspection of all the franchises throughout the country. Several years ago, however, this job had been given to a different department for a reason that had been lost in the sands of time. Robert proposed to and convinced management that the inspection job be reassigned to him, because he was the most qualified person. By accomplishing this objective, he changed his job environment with constant travel and no longer remained in his office for any length of time.

A CHANGE OF JOB STATUS

This category includes changes from line to staff position, or from full-time to part-time status, or to consulting status. It also includes job-sharing arrangements.

Jennifer S. worked for her state's health department as an insurance specialist. She decided to start a family, but wanted to remain at her job on a part-time basis. She proposed that recent budget cutbacks, her knowledge and experience with the department, and her special expertise would be most economically utilized if she worked part-time. The department enthusiastically accepted her proposal as an ideal solution to its own problem.

A CHANGE IN REPORTING STRUCTURE

You may find yourself reporting to a person who knows very little about your job and has no way of evaluating your effectiveness. Such organizational quirks can and must be corrected.

Roger T. was comptroller for the parts department of a large car dealership. His boss was the vice-president in charge of parts and had no knowledge of accounting. This arrangement made it very difficult for Roger to prove his value in order to get a raise.

His objective to be resituated under the supervision of the treasurer was accepted with relief by his boss (who disliked dealing with accounting problems), and the treasurer was more than happy to have a new staff member.

One you have a clear picture of your goal, "reality-test" it. Discuss it, *strictly off-the-record*, with one or more members of your C/I Network. You may receive either a positive or a negative reaction. If others react any way but positively, find out how you have to modify your plan of action to maximize your chances of success.

The fact that you want to bring about a change in your work situation so badly that you can taste it will give you the energy to pursue and achieve your goal, but it isn't a reliable guide to whether or not your goal is reasonable. You need someone else's detached point of view. As you'll see later, preparing a written presentation is another excellent reference point to the feasibility of your objective.

One word of advice: Don't start with a big, complex goal. Learn to walk before you run.

Be sure, also, to consider in advance the effect of achieving your desired goal on your life as a whole, on your family, and your social life, especially if a different level of involvement or change in working hours is involved.

If, for instance, a promotion to sales manager, as in Daniel D.'s case, means frequent trips out of town, consider how this will work with your life style. In Daniel's situation, his work on an MBA degree in the evening had to stop in order to take the promotion. He decided the new position, and its time demands, was worthwhile at this point in his career and postponed the work on his MBA.

Finally, be aware of the impact your objective has on your associates in your immediate work environment. Everything you do, every move you make, and any change in your work status will be known by those around you and will cause at least some slight reaction. If you receive a deserved promotion, for instance, your coworkers will congratulate you. If in their view it was undeserved, they may sharpen their knives behind your back! Make sure you consider, as a normal human relations precaution, how the achievement of your objective will affect others.

None of these caveats is intended to deter you from making your move, but to help you to plan your strategy in such a way that you remove all possible roadblocks in advance. After all, the alternative is to do nothing, which is always the worst option.

One of the consequences of doing nothing, of having no goals, is the recently much-talked-about syndrome of job burnout. Burnout isn't the complex psychological conundrum that's been advertised. It's an alignment problem. Except in extreme cases, burnout isn't brought about by overwork or stress in general. It is the result of too much of the wrong kind of work, or a moderate amount of work that's *dead wrong*. There are people who can hardly get enough of the kind of work they are physically, mentally, and spiritually in tune with, and who strive on the positive stress (also called excitement) of that kind of work.

Let's take another look at the common denominator of all your possible choices: *working and liking it*. That means that the process of change and the goals to be achieved must be tailored to your unique personality and to your personal values. At the same time, your long-range or short-range personal goals must fit the "personality" of the organization in which you function. That's true, incidentally, even if you own the organization.

A "realistic" goal for bringing about changes in your job is, by definition, one that benefits both you and your employer. It's up to you to take the initiative in setting your goals and objectives and staying in control as you implement them.

As an example, if you are a successful salesperson, and your future goal is to train other salespeople, your employer may feel that he will lose your certain ability to produce sales while taking a chance on your being able to train others. A realistic intermediate step would be for you to help one or even several other salespeople to become more productive while sustaining your own level of sales. Your employer would then know that promoting you to sales trainer, while satisfying your needs, would also benefit him. You have taken the risk out of the decision.

The wide range of possible goals includes, at one end, moving all the way to the top of an organization in the shortest time and, at the other end, creating a harmonious working relationship in your job through dependable completion of assigned duties.

There is frequently at least a small area of divergence between your ideal goal and your employer's needs. You may have to consider making small compromises. But do not accept the permanence of any condition that interferes with your enthusiasm for your work. There is always a next step or an alternative.

The achievement of the ideal job is not a fixed point in time but a process. You can always get closer. If the process generates too many negative feelings in you, if the compromises are too great, then you may be in the wrong work environment. Here are examples of two different types of compromise:

Rebecca S. started her new employment as administrative assistant to the president of a small advertising firm with the understanding that because of her lack of experience and maturity, her title would be "Administrator." At the job for over six months, she started getting agitated over the constant references to her as the "president's secretary." She also felt the president was perfectly comfortable with this assumption by the other staff members and took advantage of it by having her do an increasing number of menial errands.

Rebecca had basically good feelings about her boss and liked the administrative functions she performed. Getting closer to her ideal position would mean eliminating the menial tasks she disliked and clearly establishing herself as an administrator. In view of her goal to improve her position, the temporary compromises she had to make, such as preparing coffee and answering telephones, seemed acceptable to her.

As opposed to Rebecca, Gerry T., a systems engineer, felt there was no purpose in remaining with his present employer. Responsible for product development for a computer firm, he was in constant conflict with his boss. They not only disagreed about designs for products, they also had basic differences about the direction the company should follow. Gerry had initially hoped to increase his stock participation in the company, but he now felt there was no purpose in doing so. He firmly believed that the company was headed for disaster.

Gerry disliked his boss personally and also felt he could never respect his business judgments. Even worse, the president of the firm supported Gerry's boss in all his decisions. Gerry felt the compromises—implementing designs he felt were inferior and working late to meet unrealistic deadlines—were too great.

You may ask at this point:

"How do I know in advance what is a reasonable goal and what isn't? How can I guarantee that it would make me like my work more? After all, a promotion to a position of vast responsibility may turn out to be just an albatross around my neck later on. A transfer to another, more interesting line of work may be just a case of 'the grass is always greener. . . .'"

There is one way to be certain—perform an Achievement Analysis on yourself. Simply stated, this method allows you to establish a clear guideline for yourself, against which any job or activity you engage in, or plan to engage in, can be measured.

Here is a step-by-step outline of an Achievement Analysis:

1. On several sheets of paper, write down a minimum of ten to fifteen of the greatest achievements in your life. Include any achievements that gave you a feeling of satisfaction at the time they happened, regardless of the phase of your life in which they happened—childhood, school, work, service, avocation, religious, or recreational activity, etc. For each achievement, describe in detail *what* you did, *how* you did it, and the outcome.
2. After you've finished the list of your greatest achievements, underline any words or phrases that describe the skills, talents, or abilities you used in these achievements.

Here are a few typical examples of achievements:

While still in college, I created a private preschool summer program for children in my home town. I persuaded the park & recreations commissioner to allow me to use the town's facilities and advertised the program in the local newspapers. I successfully recruited fourteen children and hired a high school girl to assist me for the summer. All the parents said I provided a great learning experience for the kids and were particularly impressed with the music and art aspect of the program. I made a good profit and used it to go to Europe the following summer.

As administrative assistant to the vice-president of marketing for a national food franchising concern, I started a marketing news bulletin. The bulletin was distributed to 220 franchise operators and contained product information as well as advertising and marketing news from the company. I wrote and edited the entire bulletin, often <u>interviewing</u> many of the senior executives in the company to get information. The bulletin is credited now as the most valuable <u>communication</u> tool the company has for reaching its franchise owners.

I was treasurer for my church organization for two years and succeeded in simplifying the <u>bookkeeping procedures.</u> This made it possible to <u>reduce our fee</u> to the accountant, as well as to provide <u>easily understood</u> figures-at-a-glance to any member.

I also <u>convinced</u> the group to invest some of its funds in order to get a <u>higher yield on their dollars</u> than in a savings account. During my period in office, I managed to <u>reduce our operating cost</u> while <u>increasing our earnings.</u>

3. Copy all the underlined words or phrases on a separate sheet of paper.
4. Rewrite them in order of importance *to you*, starting with the most important. These are your <u>unique personal skills.</u> Any work or activity that allows you to use these skills is, by definition, right for you.

This process may seem very subjective, but it is remarkably accurate!

To illustrate the use of Achievement Analysis in setting specific goals and objectives, let's return to the story of Howard G. (told at the beginning of this chapter):

Howard moved from his position as product development specialist into sales training. His Achievement Analysis gave him a personal understanding of his greatest capabilities. It also provided him with evidence to show how he could use his skills to help his employer achieve success. Here's how Howard described his three greatest achievements:

1. As a manufacturer's representative for a business machine company, I *developed* one of my accounts to become the company's largest customer. I used my technical knowledge to *teach* the customer how to make full use of our equipment, and was able to *convince* him to use our line exclusively. Within a year, sales to this one customer increased by 200 percent.

2. When I was thirteen, I *managed* four paper routes and *increased the number of customers* for each route. After successfully working on one route for a year, and getting numerous commendations from my customers, the newspaper company asked me to *recruit* other kids for routes in surrounding neighborhoods. I *persuaded* three friends to take the jobs and told the company I'd be responsible for covering all the routes on sick days and vacations. I *negotiated* a 20 percent override on the extra routes and *trained* my friends so well that the company paid me to train all the new kids they hired in my area.

3. As owner of a franchise printing shop, I *sold* our service to three large business accounts. These accounts provided 70 percent of our business in the first year. On the basis of our reputation with these three companies, I was able to *sell* five new business accounts the following year.

In reviewing these and other achievements, it was obvious to Howard that persuading, selling, and training were essential components of his successes. Furthermore, he loved using these skills. His objective to become sales trainer was a natural next step for Howard.

The other essential consideration in defining your goal is compatibility with the "personality" and overall purpose of the organization that employs you. How does what you want to do benefit the company? This would be an easy question to answer, if our emotions didn't sometimes play tricks on us. We can always rationalize any goal we think is right for us.

Nancy R. started working as regional marketing supervisor for a national lingerie firm with the goal of getting some of her own fashion ideas in the product line. Eight months into the job, Nancy could show successful sales figures and had already developed good rapport with her superiors and subordinates. She felt the time was right to make a pitch to establish a mail order department. It seemed obvious and reasonable to her that her firm would want to expand its market.

Her achievements gave evidence of creative marketing talent. With a polished presentation and plenty of material to back up her objective, Nancy was surprised at the lack of response she got from her superiors. Unfortunately, she had failed to research the company's purposes. They did not include expanding or changing the nature of marketing their products. Her objective and presentation were developed in a vacuum and fell on deaf ears.

The lesson is clear: Reality isn't what your employer *ought* to want, but what he *wants*. If your employer's purposes aren't clear to you, or if they seem irrational, contradictory, or just plain muddleheaded, you should do the exercise outlined below to get a more realistic picture of your work environment.

1. Draw up an organizational chart to be sure you are familiar with the structure of the part of the organization that relates directly to your job. In larger companies a printed organizational diagram is often available. But beware: Printed charts frequently

only show theoretical reporting lines. Your own observations and information from your coworkers often tell you that the real lines of communication are different from the ones drawn on the "official" chart. You can then draw in the "unofficial," but real lines of who reports to whom.

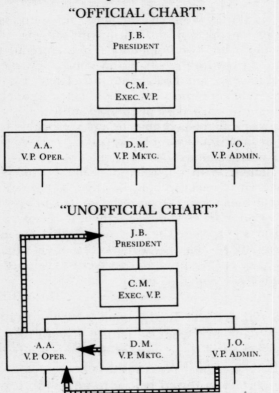

"OFFICIAL CHART"

"UNOFFICIAL CHART"

As the unofficial chart shows, the real reporting (heavy) lines bypass the ineffective executive vice-president, whose role has been taken over by the V.P. of operations.

2. To sharpen your awareness of the people environment in which you work, make a short list of the four or five key people with whom you interact dai-

ly. On paper, describe their personalities in as much detail as you can, including their greatest strengths, abilities, interests, avocations, and weaknesses (only in so far as they affect your interaction with them). A fringe benefit of this exercise is that the more you know about people, the easier it is to deal with them.

Here is an example of such a list:

Key Associates of Irving L., Operations Supervisor:
Jerry S., manager of operations (my boss), is a very self-confident, likable person. He's good on follow-up, comfortable with his authority, and politically well connected in the company. He's been with the firm for eighteen years and is probably its most loyal employee. His only weakness is that he can't delegate well and ends up doing too many menial tasks himself. He loves boating and jazz music.

Charlene T., my boss's secretary, is very detail oriented, always efficient, and presents a very professional appearance. I can always count on her to accurately communicate messages to my boss. She has more business and administrative ability than she is willing to admit and often lets others take credit for her own ideas. Her greatest weakness is her modesty and total lack of assertiveness on the job. She loves to play tennis, and is a constant party giver.

Ronald R., the company's purchasing agent, is well-known outside the firm for his bargaining and negotiating skills. He is considered valuable in the company but is not well liked. He is a health nut and a jogger and considered a little strange by some of the other top executives.

Wally Z., the company's chief accountant, is extremely dependable, always honest, and thought to be top notch in his field. Everyone likes him, but he has very little political influence in the company. His major weakness is his inability to make good hiring decisions for his department, which has a very rapid turnover. His interests are mostly his religious organization and golf.

3. Start to develop your own Contact/Information (or C/I) Network. This is a simple and elegant way to collect all the information you need to be, in a very real sense, a participant in the organization's plans, decisions, actions, and benefits.

A C/I Network is an informal group of people who pass along to you any information that makes you immediately knowledgeable about trends in the organization, about decisions made or imminent, about personnel and business changes that have taken place or are about to take place, and about opportunities available to you or dangers threatening you.

Chances are you already are part of such a network, but you probably haven't identified it and therefore aren't making the best use of it. Besides the tangible benefits of building a personal C/I Network, it will also insure that you remain in tune with the whole organization, grow with it, and are considered a valuable member of the team, *whatever your level within the organization.* In chapter 4 we'll give you detailed information on how to maximize the benefits of your C/I Network.

These useful tools, as well as the process of developing them, will sharpen your awareness of your people environment. Remember, your own goals must be compatible with the goals of the organization, and your "unofficial" organization diagram will enable you to determine who is involved in developing these goals. Your key personality descriptions will sharpen your awareness of the "players" involved. Use your Contact/Information Network to check the accuracy of your perception of these people. Roland J.'s experience illustrates the purpose and use of a Contact/Information Network:

As manager of product development for a consumer goods company, he frequently proposed concepts for new products at board of directors' meetings. Each of these proposals was crucial to achieving his personal career goals.

Preliminary research to prepare for these presentations often tied up Roland's staff for weeks at a time. When new product ideas were completely rejected, his reputation as a realistic and innovative product developer was threatened. Also, his staff members would feel shot down and would sometimes be unproductive for days.

It was clear to Roland that he had to have a better idea of the product expectations and interests of the board of directors before his proposals could succeed. Through his C/I Network, Roland learned that one member of the board of directors strongly influenced every decision made by the group. So Roland found out as much as he could about this board member and then tackled him in person. The director welcomed Roland's genuine interest in his productive development philosophy and was pleased to share his views. The conversation completely removed any roadblocks, resulting in successful product proposals from then on.

Rule of Thumb: As long as any of your superiors' purposes seem mysterious or irrational to you, you haven't completed your preliminary research process. At this point you need to clearly understand the environment of which you are a part. You may not always agree with your employer's goals and ideas—you may either like or dislike them—but you must know what they are so you can accurately assess the size of the compromises you may have to make. For instance:

> Herbert T., a high school science teacher, disagreed with the department head on almost all policies. Herbert was sure this man was just sticking around long enough to collect his pension, and he only made policy decisions that wouldn't ruffle any feathers.
>
> Herbert had been attempting to introduce new curriculum material and requested a minor increase in his budget for experimentation equipment. He received no such increase and chalked it up to his superior's basic lack of support or interest. The relationship between the two men became increasingly tense, and Herbert considered looking for a job in a more progressive school.
>
> There was little or no communication between Herbert and his boss for quite some time. Finally, Herbert discovered through his C/I Network that his boss was *not* simply motivated by a desire to "stick it out" until retirement. By asking his boss the right questions, Herbert finally found him to be encouraging and supportive. Herbert learned that his educational concepts and proposals had been rejected simply because of a school deficit of which he had previously been unaware.
>
> Without this research, Herbert would have continued to base his own career decisions on wrong assumptions about his employer. With accurate information about his superior's goals and ideas, and the knowledge that the school's deficit would be resolved in six months, he was able to solicit adequate support to implement a successful long-range program for curriculum changes in his department.

These examples show the importance of the Contact/Information process. In the next chapter we'll give you step-by-step instructions for building your own C/I Network.

CHAPTER 4

BUILDING AND USING A CONTACT/ INFORMATION NETWORK

The idea of Contact/Information Networks is not new. All of us are members of such networks practically from the time when we start to communicate with others.

As schoolchildren our networks included parents, relatives, our teachers, the family's friends, the family doctor and dentist; kids who had the same hobby, members of clubs we belonged to, and our own friends.

As adults, even if we don't have a paying job, we know a score of professionals who provide us with personal services, we have social circles, we may know people through volunteer work, and we have contact with people who are interested in the same sports or other avocations. Even if you've lived a very sheltered life, building a network is a natural and easy thing to do.

We have seen that the enjoyment of work as well as

career advancement depend on good information about the organizations in which we work. The best way to get this information is to build and maintain your own personal Contact/Information Network— (C/I Network).

In this chapter we'll define the concept and give you the ground rules for building your C/I Network. We'll start by explaining what a C/I Network is and what it isn't.

A Contact/Information Network is a *human* resource and information exchange system. It allows you to tap into a vast reservoir of knowledge about practically everybody and everything.

Identifying members of a C/I Network is the same as identifying any other resources available to you. They're always there, but are of value to you only if you recognize and use them productively, just as you make your knowledge, information, and insights available to others who recognize their value.

Only productive, successful, and emotionally positive associates qualify for membership in your C/I Network. Unsuccessful people, by definition, can't help you, and are more likely to drag you into negative trends and relationships.

Only constructive information must be given and asked for. Obviously, bad news is occasionally exchanged, but solely for the purpose of taking constructive action, which ultimately benefits both you and your employer. We most emphatically do not encourage building or being part of a gossip network!

You may hear from a coworker: "I have information that the company may be going out of business." This bad news is not necessarily gossip. This kind of information, properly checked out, may put you in a position to make a constructive plan of action in the event that the company *does* go out of business.

On the other hand, for instance, if someone you work with said, "I hear the boss's wife has a drinking problem," you've got gossip on your hands. This information is totally useless to building positive and constructive relationships or plans for advancement.

All constructive communication consists of give and take. You are a member of the C/I Network of every person who is a part of yours. *All human interaction is reciprocal.* You will be seeing this phrase throughout this book. As I am to you, so you are to me. It's probably the one most important principle we'll be talking about. Properly understood, it can be the single rule that guides you securely throughout your career.

Through your C/I Network, as we have seen, you may also learn of decisions or attitudes that can affect your position adversely. If, for instance, you discover lack of support or value for any functions you are performing, you will have good warning from your C/I Network to seek new and more appropriate tasks within your organization.

When you give good and relevant information to members of your C/I Network, you will get the same in return. The more others within this Network perceive you as a valuable member of the Information system, the more good and relevant information will come your way.

The knowledge that is shared by members of a C/I Network is assumed by most employees to be communicated through official channels. This would theoretically be ideal but is rarely the case. Valuable information that you may exchange with your C/I Network includes:

- Financial decisions that may affect your job
- Opportunities that may occur when someone is leaving the organization or when a new department is being created

- Knowledge about a merger or acquisition that may be on the horizon
- Customer feedback on a product or service of your organization
- Information about a person you don't get along with—which allows you to establish a better relationship.

Information from your C/I Network can give insight into new needs that may arise in the organization, providing you with opportunities to increase your responsibility, change the direction of your position, or change jobs completely.

When you are clear on your goals and objectives, the information you receive from your C/I Network can be easily translated into opportunities. You will discover that you become much "luckier" at achieving your objectives!

For instance, if you've been waiting for the "right time" to ask for a raise, information that your firm has been awarded a valuable new contract will translate into the "golden opportunity" to ask for a salary increase.

Jonathan O., an insurance underwriter, heard through his C/I Network that the manager of his department, Ben, was up for a promotion. Jonathan already was on a good footing with his boss but had never shared his ideas for improving the department's procedures and increasing efficiency.

Jonathan used this information about Ben's promotion to his advantage by speedily preparing his ideas and presenting them to him. When Ben got promoted, he recommended Jonathan as a replacement for himself.

Here is a step-by-step guide to building your C/I Network:

1. Make a list of all the people who are in key positions in the company, whom you know well, and with whom you enjoy free and open communications. There may only be one or two people on this list. Never mind, it's a start.
2. Add to this list the names of all people in responsible or key positions whom you know slightly, but would like to build a better or closer talking relationship with.
3. Now add the people whom you consider essential to your C/I Network, but with whom you are not acquainted or with whom you haven't communicated in the past beyond minimum daily courtesy. (Note: People in decision-making positions have priority, but your peers or people below your level can be important sources of information about areas of the organization about which you know very little and vice versa).

Keep communication channels open with your current C/I Network members. Talk to them *every day,* however briefly. And start communicating with new C/I recruits, avoiding idle chatter. Beyond normal courtesies, your conversation should focus on the company's business or the other person's strengths and interests.

Once you start this process, you'll never stop. You'll find that anything you want to achieve in your work, whether it is happiness, change, or advancement, will be *directly* dependent on the strength and quality of your C/I Network. What's more, eventually you will expand your network beyond the limits of your present organization to include key people in your profession as a whole. You'll also be building, almost without being aware of it, a C/I Network in your life outside of your work.

Here is an example of a Contact/Information Network list prepared by a research coordinator for a financial investment firm:

1. *People I Know Well:*
   My Boss, the Director of Corporate Services
   The Director of Research
   Research Coordinator for Capital Goods
2. *People I Need to Know Better:*
   Institutional Marketing Director
   Vice-President, Real Estate Investment Program
   Vice-President, Marketing
   Individual Portfolio Manager
3. *People in My Firm Who Should Become a Part of My C/I Network:*
   Executive Committee members
   (they make final decisions on total investment packages)
   Vice-President, Investment Management Service
   The President of my firm
4. *Outside My Firm:*
   The President of H.S.B. Corp., a small new firm
   The lawyer who represents my firm
   President of Thorpe Co., a large investor with our firm
   Mr. Higgins, a major investor

Here is another C/I Network list, for a graphic artist at a small advertising agency:

1. *People I Know Well:*
   My Boss, the Art Director
   Janice, the Media Buyer
   The Publicity Director
2. *People I Need to Know Better:*
   Harold, the company President
   The President of A&G Eyeglasses (a major account)
   The two account executives for our firm

3. *People in My Firm Who Should Become a Part of My C/I Network:*
   The Vice-President of Market Research
   The Senior Copywriter
4. *Outside My Firm:*
   The President of Clothes Unlimited (another account of the firm)
   The Art Director at RZ Advertising Co.
   The directors who are members of the Ad Club

The temptation toward negative uses of your C/I Network will sometimes be irresistible. In times of stress, we all need somebody to commiserate with our problems, to help us identify the guilt of others, to listen to our complaints, to share inside "dirt" with.

It sometimes takes willpower to resist the temptation to contaminate your C/I Network with negative information. The risk is that, eventually, you will no longer receive information of value from former network members, even though they seemed sympathetic to your problems at the time.

The receiver of negative information is likely to accept it, and will probably even agree with you. However, that person will ignore you in the future because he sees you as having a negative attitude and you might even spread gossip about him.

Example: "John is up for a promotion, but I think it would be a disaster for the firm. I heard he's having trouble with his marriage. There have even been some rumors that one of his children is on drugs."

On the other hand, there are great benefits from being identified as a trustworthy, discreet, constructive person by senior members of your organization. You'll be given confidential information often and early enough to put you in control of your job, your work environment, and your career.

In addition to your C/I Network, specific mentors can sometimes be a valuable resource to you. A mentor is a person you choose as a personal adviser or role model. However, our experience tells us that there are some dangers to avoid. The single mentor is often a disaster because you're tempted to put all your eggs in one basket. Only successful people can help you to be successful! Because there are many ways to be successful, a Contact/Information Network of successful people is far more useful than a lone mentor. Yet, many people single out one person within their organization and appoint him or her as their mentor. They crash to the floor when their mentor turns out to have "feet of clay" or leaves the organization altogether.

Gail M.'s case illustrates this point. As far as she was concerned, the only reason she got promoted to production supervisor at her radio station was because of the station's manager. She had worked as his secretary for two years and attributed her career growth to the fact that "he recognized I had talent and encouraged me to grow. He's completely responsible for putting me in the job I have now."

Unfortunately, her boss left the station and was replaced by a new manager shortly after Gail got her promotion. At this point Gail's career started to decline. Instead of doing production work, she was gradually relegated to a series of menial jobs. Since that time, her attitude about the job has been "I knew it would be downhill after my first boss left. He was the only one who cared about me. I'm not sure how long I'll last here without him."

Instead of establishing a relationship with her new boss, Gail used most of her energy to mourn the departure of her old boss.

This example isn't meant to deter you from considering mentors or role models altogether. The final example in this chapter shows that the more human resources you identify and the more use you make of them, the more positive control you will have over your work environment.

Stephen M. used multiple mentors. As a high school English teacher, he determined that his growth as an educator would require sharpening his skills in classroom discipline techniques, developing expertise in his subject, and learning how to work creatively within a curriculum. For each of these areas, he developed relationships with different people.

His resource for honing his classroom skills was a veteran teacher in his school. Stephen also developed a close relationship with the school principal, who gave him insight into curriculum development and application. His third mentor was one of his old college instructors with whom he enjoyed discussing literature in great detail.

Each of his mentors provided different areas of expertise and counsel. All three were resources he used for his professional development and valuable additions to his own C/I Network.

Now that you are fully in charge of your own "Human Resource Development" (you've probably always wondered what that term meant!), you are ready for the next step: taking control of your entire job environment.

CHAPTER 5

CONTROLLING YOUR JOB ENVIRONMENT

Liking your work means not only managing your job and your career, but also the environment in which you do your work. Now that you've learned how to develop an important, basic career management tool—the Contact/Information process—you are ready to look at your total job and work environment.

Managing your job, or being in control of it, first of all involves building constructive relationships with the people you work with. It does not involve clever ploys, tricks, or politics in the negative sense of putting others down. If you have any doubts, ask a few people whom you consider genuinely successful in their work and their careers. See if their statements are similar to those made by people we know:

> "I love what I do and I'm probably doing one of the top jobs in my field right now. Public affairs for hospitals has its political problems because there are so many people to account to. You have to be able to

56

make decisions and get the ball rolling *without stepping on toes.*"

"Job satisfaction is definitely 100 percent important to me. I'm in total control of my job at the moment, but I know the whole thing could be in jeopardy if the board of directors doesn't see a real value in me. I submit monthly and annual reports on my work and that of my staff because I know I have to show a bottom-line success story."

"I turned my department into a profit-making division about four years ago. It's the first time in our little company's history that this has been done."

"Being in control of my job and feeling satisfied meant that I had to create a balance between my work life and personal life. I devote a lot of time to my family, and I couldn't be happy in my work if I didn't."

"I'm not one of those people you see working into the wee hours, so I know I have to make myself visible in other ways. I keep a list of my accomplishments at all times and I have a weekly meeting with my boss to discuss them. I set up this system about a year ago, and it's helped me feel less paranoid about the clock watchers. I know I do a good job and I always have proof. My boss has been very supportive."

The common denominator of all these statements is that the people who made them appear to give a feeling of confidence, of being actively involved in and in control of their job environment.

Taking control does not mean manipulation of others for personal gain. It means actively and positively communicating with others for mutual benefit.

Being in control also does not involve compromising your values. If it does in your circumstances, you will have to ask yourself the crucial question: "Should I be working here?" Quitting your job is always an option, but it should never be the first option.

Controlling your job environment means nothing more nor less than having a goal or a purpose, and getting everyone around you to help you reach your goal and support your purpose.

If you agree that control is a prerequisite for liking your work, here are six things you can do to achieve this desirable state:

1. Make sure your work is up to your own *and* your employer's standard of quality. If it isn't, make this your first goal to be achieved before you do anything else.
2. Examine your work relationships with your superiors and others, and correct them if they are not positive.
3. Build a reputation for reliability and results.
4. Be aware of your personal appearance: mental and physical fitness as well as grooming and dress, and the attitude communicated by your appearance and behavior.
5. Find out *what* your organization does and *how* it's done.
6. Find our *why* your organization does what it does, its purposes and goals, its reason for existence.

In discussing the implementation of those six steps, we'll look at everything from two points of view: yours and others. Both must be satisfied, not one *or* the other.

Step 1. Start by taking a good look at your work from those two points of view. In terms of quality, is it up to your own expectations and those of your superiors? Are you behind schedule?

You may have a problem here. The whole reason for doing something about your work is that there are aspects of it you can't stand. How can anyone expect you to do a good job under those circumstances?

Yet how can you motivate your superiors to help you bring about a change for the better if they see you as a failure? Why should they recognize your value and give you greater opportunities if they perceive you as not even able to do the job you've got?

The solution is simple: You must put yourself into a position of strength as a precondition for any forward move.

The following example shows how this can be done:

Milton Q., manager of one sporting goods store in a chain, wanted to become operations manager for the entire chain.

Although his capabilities suited his goal well, Milton was doing a poor job in his present position. In fact, he found taking inventory and spending any time in the store's stockroom so distasteful that he ignored the merchandising aspects of retail management altogether. He soon found his store doing poorly and rapidly gained a reputation as a below-average store manager.

With this history, Milton was not in any position to make a case for a promotion to manager of operations for the chain. Nevertheless, he felt his retail experience, his product knowledge, and the ability to train and supervise staff were sufficient evidence of his potential to do the job.

His boss didn't think so. He, in fact, took the opportunity to tell Milton that he must move his stock out on the sales floor. Milton had the authority to reduce prices, but the stock had to move. Determined to be seen as good management material and to achieve his goal, Milton put aside his hatred for stockroom work and virtually locked himself in for three days. He got the stock out on the floor, repriced it, advertised it, and sold it.

In overcoming his specific weakness as perceived by his boss, Milton removed the obstacle to his promotion. As long as he was perceived as ineffective, no goal was realistic.

Step 2. Next, examine your relationship with your boss. No one has ever found this easy. What do you think about your boss? How do you feel about your boss? How does he/she feel about you, at least so far as you know?

You don't have to be a psychologist. If you find it difficult to communicate with your boss on a daily basis, you have a problem that needs correcting. Human relations problems with your boss can range from not being exactly on the same wavelength, or not knowing a lot about each other, to deep, seemingly unbridgeable personality conflicts, as the following examples illustrate:

> A bookkeeper at a publishing firm states, "My boss is picky about details and never open to new ideas. No one really knows what he's thinking. He never tells us anything. I think he's really paranoid. He has repeatedly shot down my ideas, so I know he doesn't like me. I don't feel comfortable talking to him about anything anymore—so we just don't talk."

> A marketing consultant say, "I simply don't like the way my boss does business. He has a really obnoxious attitude about our customers and is always mocking them behind their backs. I think he intimidates most of them into using our ideas, instead of selling them on the real value of what we have to offer. I think he's getting very jealous of me because a lot of the customers like me.

> "I don't know how long I can stand working here. Putting up with my boss's ego is getting to be impossible."

Where do you start in correcting a personality conflict? And why should *you* be the one to take the initiative? After all, if it's not your fault that you don't get along well, why should you make all the effort?

Let's stop a moment and take the opportunity to kick the word "fault" into oblivion. It's the single most dangerous roadblock to taking positive action.

Let's replace "fault" with "responsibility." Something may not be your fault, but it may be your responsibility to correct it—if you want the results that will be produced by doing so.

Claudia T. was in constant conflict with her boss, who she felt was a die-hard male chauvinist. Her initial response to most of his personal communication with her was pure disgust. As the tension between them increased, Claudia recognized that she'd lose her job if she didn't control her own reactions. By focusing on the more bearable aspects of her boss's personality, she actually found some common ground. Ultimately Claudia discovered that with the tension removed, she made more impact on her boss's chauvinistic tendencies by just being liked, being there, and doing a good job.

All communications roadblocks must be removed before you can manage your human work environment. Here is a way to do this:

Start by focusing your mind on the new, *positive trend* you are going to build. Ignore all the emotional baggage produced by the negative history of your past relationship. Make a list of any and all of your boss's abilities, talents, work and life achievements, positive character traits, and major personal interests. Everybody has them. For the purpose of this exercise, *don't* try to be objective—be positive, even if it's not always easy. If you want to learn to take control of human relationships, resist the powerful pull of negative emotional habits.

You may find that you don't have enough positive information about your boss to even get started on your list. Okay, take a little time to find out. After you have finished your list, you will not, alas, love your boss. That may never happen, and it wasn't the purpose of the exercise. But you *will* have a more emotionally balanced picture of him or her and, what's more important, you will have a point of departure for your future constructive relationship.

Here's one positive boss profile:

Punctual
Follows through on promises
Good with details
Gives credit where it's due
Technically competent
Politically active in his community
Donates time to charity
Good family relationships
Works energetically
Loyal to the company
Knowledgeable about stereo systems
Loves to eat at excellent restaurants
Loves music
Writes reports creatively
Believes in company's product.

Now focus on any area of strength in which you find it easy to relate to your boss. There are several ways to use the above example to open up communications in a positive, comfortable, and sincere manner. If you have a genuine interest in music, for instance, you might share some of your reactions to a particular performance or recording and ask for your boss's opinion of it.

The key is to focus on a mutual interest or area of expertise. To break the ice and start a positive emotional trend, choose only areas in which you're honestly interested. The amazing thing about this approach is that once you've started communicating positively about *anything*, you've created a path toward positive communication in your daily interactions with your boss.

If you believe strongly in your company's product, you'd be in a good position to start a positive trend with the boss in the above profile. One way to begin the process would be to discuss new ways of promoting or improving the product.

To remove the boulders of negative or downright destructive interpersonal relations from your work path may sound cumbersome and time consuming. It isn't! After you've done it a few times, it will become a habit. In fact, you will find that it becomes so natural that you won't allow relationships to deteriorate in the first place. Instead you will have developed a subconscious sensing and correcting mechanism that will function whenever you interact with people.

After you have corrected any problems in your relationships with your superiors, apply the same methods to relationships with your peers and subordinates. Having accomplished this, you will have taken the first and most important step towards controlling and liking your work.

Here is the real fringe benefit of taking positive action in interpersonal relations:

Mel K. and Douglas V.'s case is a good illustration of this primary step toward job happiness. The two worked side by side as draftsmen for a small electronic consulting firm. Mel was an ultraliberal and active political organizer, while Douglas was ultraconservative and quite vocal about his political views. Unfortunately, they couldn't seem to keep politics from becoming the focus of their contact with each other. When it got to the point where they were calling each other names and visibly moving toward the lunatic fringe, Mel took a step. He invited Douglas to lunch, and after establishing a mood of congeniality, got Douglas's commitment to avoid political discussions from then on.

Positive action results in positive reaction. Smile and people smile back. Show sincere interest and concern for those in your work environment, and you'll find that you have the power to set the tone for those around you.

Step 3. Now that your work is in good shape and your relationships with your boss and other key associates are either positive or getting there, you're ready to work on developing a reputation for reliability, cooperation, follow-through, and results!

Every organization has a few people who stand out because no matter what task they are given, they produce results on time and within budget and other predetermined limits. The level of the person is immaterial, as is the size or importance of the task. It may be typing a letter, making a phone call, or managing a $10 million project.

Having a choice of being given the right tasks has to be earned. An actor is not in a position to turn down movie scripts when none are offered. His first step is to prove acting ability.

In order to establish a reputation for doing anything, you must first do it. Preferably several times. Fortunately this is the easiest part of gaining control of your work environment. Take the initiative to volunteer for tasks that are compatible with your skills and abilities. As long as the projects make a genuine contribution to the organization, your initiative will always be welcome. Make reasonable promises and keep them. There are a wealth of opportunities.

If, for instance, your job and skill areas include marketing, you may be in a position to identify and fulfill a variety of organizational needs. If you should determine that sales and product image could be boosted by a new brochure, you might propose to develop, write, or edit one. The important thing is to be sure you are in line with the thinking of your superiors before you take on the task, and once you've started the project, follow through.

The procedure is basically to identify a need, check its validity with your superiors, and execute the job with consistently high performance.

We know many people who have successfully altered their jobs to meet their personal interests by using this approach.

An engineer who enjoyed writing technical material identified a company's need for accurately written brochures to promote and describe its products. His writing ability, combined with his technical expertise, enabled him to create a position for himself as promotional director for a high-tech firm.

A television producer who wanted to develop new features for a weekly talk show carefully studied public interest polls, proposed features in line with her findings, and developed a reputation for consistently increasing the show's ratings. Her performance in this area enabled her to become an executive producer.

Remember, your objective is not to generate a fantastic amount of motion, noise, and busywork. Your purpose is to demonstrate by positive action that you are a responsible person and can be trusted to produce results under a variety of circumstances. By logical extension, this leads to being given a wider range of assignments and opportunities for growth, with the resulting increase in choice and control which are a necessary prerequisite for liking your work.

Step 4. To put the icing on the cake and to remove any remaining roadblocks to your free exercise of choice in your work environment, give some thought to your personal appearance. How do others see you, how do you feel about yourself? Everyone agrees that dress is an important factor; bookstores do a thriving business in this area alone.

The fact is that people react on the visual level to the way you dress and to your apparent state of physical fitness. They also react, on the emotional level, to the attitude you seem to be projecting through your appearance. You need to be aware of both these reactions.

However visually interesting, a person whose appearance is in conflict with his environment is felt to be out of tune—at best of not wanting to make the effort, at worst of rebellion. A person projecting a poor physical condition is creating an emotional climate of poor quality, problems, and nonproductivity.

Eric E., for instance, a shoe salesman for a swank fashion-oriented shoe salon, had played with the thought of becoming a buyer. Although Eric was a successful salesman, he was judged only on the basis of his personal appearance. Always dragging himself around like he'd had a sleepless night, wearing clothes that looked a size too large, and generally looking undernourished, Eric did not present the appearance of a dynamic salesperson or an up-and-coming fashion buyer. No matter how much he was able to accomplish in his job, he never seemed to be able to favorably impress his boss.

Because the assumed underlying attitude is the key factor in matters of personal appearance, this should be your starting point. Instead of beginning with external considerations—of matching suit, dress, and accessories, of whether to acquire a real suntan or to get it out of a bottle—decide what *attitude* you wish to project. And make sure that this attitude is in tune with your real personality.

If you want to project energy, your posture, the way you walk, and even the way you sit will have an effect on the way others perceive you. In the words of one employer: "If he walks and sits slumped over, his work is probably slumped over."

If, on the other hand, you're in a career position which requires you to project a cool, collected, and understated image, such as a management consultant, you would not walk, talk, stand, or wish to appear as a super-energy person would, such as a sales manager.

To develop and be at ease with your image requires an analysis of your career environment, as well as an honest look at how you fit into it and the way you'd like to be perceived.

Barbara A., for instance, was an aspiring executive in a cosmetics firm. Although many of the so-called experts insisted that successful women executives should wear grey flannel business suits, she had determined from her own observations that soft, feminine, and floral were generally the choice of the successful top female executives in *her* firm. Already comfortable with her choice of clothing, Barbara now worked toward improving her figure through exercise and achieving the appearance of high energy that was also a hallmark of the top executives.

The ground rule for dress is: Be in tune with the organization in which you work. No more and no less. This is not an invitation to be as inconspicuous as possible. Observation over a period of time will give you a good sense of what is the right way to dress. Until you have developed it, take your cue from the most successful of your associates.

With regard to health, it's important to remember that extremes of any kind create obstacles in your relationships with others. The emotional climate surrounding a grossly overweight person is one such obstacle. Interestingly, and in accordance with the advice given above, losing weight is not the only solution to this problem.

Take into account the general prejudices that relate to body types. Just as people may assume that thin, wiry types are high energy people, those carrying above-average weight are supposed to be lethargic or lazy.

One man we know had a problem with subordinates who assumed he wasn't able to accomplish the goals of his marketing position. As director of a highly energetic sales force, his overweight appearance automatically seemed to indicate a lack of ability to perform quickly, responsively, and with the kind of vitality his sales force expected.

In actuality, this marketing director was a highly energetic, physically active individual. He owned and drove a racing car in competition. He also had a pilot's license and enjoyed horseback riding. This information, once he shared it with others in his company, helped to promote his image as an active, fast-moving person.

Step 5. After considering and starting to work on mutual perceptions in your immediate day-to-day relationships, turn your attention to the larger picture: the organization you work in.

In order to manage your job, to like your work, to advance and grow, get to know how the total organization works and why it works the way it does. Find out how decisions are made, who makes them, what those decisions are or will be, and how they affect you. In other words, learn how you fit into the total picture. Without that knowledge you can have no freedom of movement and your capacity for work enjoyment is limited.

Start by asking yourself if you know what your company actually does, and how it's done. That sounds pretty basic, but there are actually many people, especially in larger or diversified corporations, who have only the vaguest notion about their company's products or services beyond their own immediate involvement.

A clear understanding of your company's products or services, as well as the market for them, is necessary to being in tune with the goals and purposes of your superiors.

When asked what his company did, an accountant for a management consulting firm replied: "All I know is that they work with Fortune 500 companies. I'm not sure exactly what they do."

An administrator for the shipping department of a major electronics firm said, "We make some kind of parts for the computer industry. It's highly technical stuff."

A radio program producer responded, "I'm not sure what the station is really trying to do. I know who the audience is, but my boss doesn't seem to have a real marketing strategy. At least, he never talked to me about it."

Information about what your organization produces is abundantly available. Collect printed material, such as annual reports, product or services brochures, and newsletters. But above all talk with people who are involved in the various product or service areas. They will appreciate your sincere interest.

Step 6. The next and more complex task is to find out *why* your organization is in business. We all make assumptions about our boss's motivations, their personal as well as business objectives and their priorities. Most of these assumptions turn out to be inaccurate on closer observation. Here are some typical statements:

> "My boss is really just waiting to retire. He doesn't have any real goals anymore."

> "This organization has so many people involved in making decisions that, in my opinion, they've lost their focus and direction."

> "The purpose of this company changes from week to week. Every department head is really out for himself, especially my boss. It's a very disjointed company."

> "The company's only in business to make money, just like any other company."

> "Nobody really talks about what we're in business for. At least no one ever told me."

This is called a frog's-eye perspective. How is it possible to cooperate constructively in achieving a purpose that is not understood or appreciated?

Will your objective be to cooperate in achieving the purposes of the organization that employs you, or to disrupt it? Don't be offended by this question. Most people who habitually get in the way of the flow of a company's work don't do so intentionally. They simply don't understand the long-range or short-range objectives, values, and working style of their superiors and sometimes their associates. After all, nobody told them! This, in fact, is another red-flag statement.

Whenever you hear yourself saying "Nobody tells me anything," it's time to start asking questions. But whom do you ask? The first person you meet at the coffee machine?

There are people in every part of every organization who, figuratively speaking, have their finger on the pulse of the enterprise. They are either natural communicators, or they are placed in the path of accurate information by the nature of their jobs. These are the people you need to seek out and associate with. We have described in detail in chapter 4 (Building and Using a Contact/Information Network) how to identify them, cultivate them, and tell them apart from uninformed gossips.

We have all seen examples of shortcuts to personal advancement that appear to ignore all the steps described in this chapter. These include winning by intimidation, emotional blackmail, and stepping on people's toes in a rush to get to the top. For the person tempted to follow these routes, study the case histories of those who have tried it. While the short-range achievements have occasionally been spectacular, the price has been high and the long-range effects on the careers of those involved have been disastrous. Not to mention negative costs in terms of mental and physical health, private life, and marriage.

Robert C.'s background was in mechanical engineering, but his major interest was business management. Arming himself with an MBA, he determined to quickly rise to the top of whatever organization he decided to join.

As a respected newcomer to the O.C. Company, makers of medical research instrumentation, Robert was placed in a design team that was responsible for a specific engineering project. The team consisted of two electronic engineers, two technicians, a draftsman, and Robert himself.

Only a few months after his arrival, Robert began to disrupt the organizational structure by insisting that the draftspeople had too little to do in the present design groups. He convinced the president of the company that a return to the traditional departmentalization of functions (electrical engineering, mechanical engineering, technicians, drafting) would provide the organization with a more cost-effective use of talent.

The president, at this point, was investing a great deal of hope and loyalty in Robert's opinions and practices. He took his advice and restructured the company. Now he felt obliged to support Robert all the way, even though the reorganization of the company had a demoralizing effect on almost every member of the original design teams.

Robert's approach to gaining control and responsibility for decision making was simply to make the decisions and assume he'd be supported by the president. For some time he was.

As he gained power, most of the engineers and draftspeople learned to distrust and dislike him. He was soon known as a hatchet man, eager to search out any "dead wood" in the organization.

Robert continued to increase his own power, seemingly undaunted, until he clashed with the president of the company, because Robert now made decisions that excluded the president.

Ultimately, Robert was booted down two levels in the organization. He left the O.C. Company less than six months later.

The six steps we've described in this chapter—1. Bringing your work up-to-date; 2. Reviewing your relationships on the job; 3. Building a reputation for reliability; 4. Sharpening your personal appearance; 5. Getting to know what your organization does; and 6. Understanding your employer's goals and purposes— show clearly that *communicating* with others is a necessity. It's an essential part of being in control of your job environment.

It should be evident that we are referring here to positive communications for constructive purposes. However, many people shoot themselves in the foot, thereby undoing all the advantages their positive communications have gained them:

We are referring to the way problems or complaints are communicated. Problems are a natural part of every organization and every job. Do you find yourself describing problems to your superiors in these terms: "I'm sick and tired of . . ." or, "I can't stand . . ." or, "I'm not going to put up with . . ."?

Here are some examples of real problems communicated by people we know:

Carol's complaint to her boss:

"Jack is impossible to work with. All of his decisions are selfishly motivated. He never seems to think of the future of the company. I feel like I only respond to crisis after crisis. With him as my assistant, I never get any real work done. I've told him repeatedly that it would be better if he didn't work that way, but he doesn't get the message."

Jim's complaint to the president of his company:

"I hate the way everyone is out for himself here. Every time we try to work as a management team, everybody acts as if they're in competition with each other. I don't see how I can advance in the organization if no one is willing to share their ideas and communicate about their projects."

Never bring a problem to anyone without suggesting a solution.

You are abdicating responsibility whenever you lodge a complaint without a remedy. You are shifting responsibility to the other person and loading the work on his or her shoulders. This is often unconscious-ly perceived as an act of hostility by the recipient of the complaint or problem, especially when it isn't part of that person's normal agenda. The ego gratification of being thought capable of dealing with the problem is small for the person so approached, and not enough to wipe out the negative impact. Repeated often, a demonstrably negative emotional trend builds up between the bearer of problems or bad news and the receiver.

You can convert the action of communicating a problem into an entirely positive event by packaging it as a solution.

If, for instance, you are responsible for designing a program with a specific budget ceiling, don't tell your boss "it can't be done." Instead, provide an outline or presentation for what can be done under the present financial constraints, and then show what might be accomplished in specific terms with more money.

If personality problems with coworkers or subordinates are creating obstacles in accomplishing given assignments, your boss won't be happy to hear that "they're impossible to work with; we can't get anything done." On the other hand, if you present a new team structure or a new proposal for task assignments, your boss will receive you as a problem solver, rather than a problem maker.

Robert C., in the earlier example, forged ahead without doing this and found himself moving *down* the organizational ladder. We propose that you suggest solutions to your boss instead of lodging complaints. But remember to get your boss's go-ahead before you implement the solutions.

Now that we've shown you how to create a positive climate for taking control of your job environment, we'll talk in more detail about the most important part of that environment: people.

CHAPTER 6

BUILDING POSITIVE WORK RELATIONSHIPS: HOW TO GET ALONG WITH NEARLY EVERYBODY

Money, profit, market shares, and productivity are all real concepts of the work world, yet none of them has any meaning without people. Your relationships with people are the key to liking your work. And communications are the key to your relationships with people.

You don't need to be a psychologist to know how to establish good relationships on the job. You just have to know and follow some simple, basic principles. We referred to some of these principles in chapter 5; we'll explain them in more detail in this chapter. The pioneering on work relationships has been done by Eli

Djeddah, author and career counselor, and thousands of people who have implemented his principles successfully.

Your goal may be to enjoy your work for eight hours every day of the week, to change your job description, or to become president of the company. Whatever your goal, you'll need the support of a number of people to reach it. Certainly you'll need your boss's support. Enjoying that support is the best example of being in control of your human environment.

Being in control may be a frightening concept to some. It may imply having to make daily decisions about what you want to happen today, where you are headed tomorrow—where you want to be five years from now. Not to worry: Being in control of your work environment is no more or less frightening than the concept of freedom. It gives you a tool, a ticket to a destination you wish to go to, *when* you are ready to go. It creates a *condition*, not an end result.

The condition of being in control helps you to know that you can do almost anything you want to do when you want to do it. Within reason! As we have seen, the limiting factor is that *whatever you want to do must benefit others as well*. Establishing control at the expense of others will not work. It's a contradiction in terms.

Janet learned this ground rule the hard way. Her goal was to create a marketing department for her organization and become the firm's first marketing director.

As special research assistant to the president of a nationwide health care consulting organization, Janet identified the need to combine the advertising efforts of the firm with the information she collected in her research activities to create a total marketing program.

At first she was highly successful in gathering support from key members of the organization. The company was in generally good financial condition, and there were no major company problems. People had the time and willingness to listen to her ideas and share theirs.

As she continued to perform the research activities requested by the president, she simultaneously gathered information to support her proposal for establishing the new marketing department. She then scheduled a series of conferences with outside marketing and computer data consultants and the key members of her company. Her aim at this point was to develop a computerized system for collecting and analyzing company research information. Up to this time, the firm had never used computers for anything outside of simple accounting procedures.

For the most part, Janet believed the key members of the company supported her goal, but she found herself increasingly frustrated when it came to communicating with the president. His research needs were simple and, to his mind, relatively unimportant. Janet felt that her reports were never put to good use. Her interest in her research activities dwindled, but she began to escalate her campaign for creating a market department.

At about this time, a number of major events occurred within the company. The key people on whom Janet depended for support and information had to concentrate their energies on getting four new branches in various parts of the country off the ground. Simultaneously, an important financial transaction fell through, leaving the organization with serious cashflow problems. Janet's support group was no longer available for spur-of-the-moment meetings and consultation. Instead, her colleagues were travelling frequently, dealing with daily personnel problems, and were preoccupied with the critical financial condition of the corporation.

Janet saw these events as further proof that her marketing concepts were essential to the success of the firm, and she forged ahead with her campaign by setting up more meetings. She notified prospective participants by memo but discovered that key members of the group were frequently unavailable or disinterested. For Janet, this was a signal of major mismanagement by the corporate staff, and a source of greater frustration to her. Her only recourse, she felt, would be to get support from the president of the company.

With intense commitment and undaunted belief in her solution for the firm's problems, Janet sent a memo to the president, carefully outlining the firm's difficulties and demanding his support for her solution.

The president's reply was a simple memo: He no longer required her services as special research assistant and requested that she prepare to leave the premises by the end of the month. As though to soften the blow, Janet thought, he included a paragraph suggesting that he would be happy to consider specific research proposals and to work with her in the future on a project basis only. She was devastated.

Janet was guilty of destructive wavemaking. She was completely out of rhythm, emotionally and factually, with the organization. At a time when key executives were putting out fires on a daily basis and worried about the company's survival, Janet was asking them to focus on *future* needs and *future* growth.

One wave created a series of other waves. Because she was out of rhythm, Janet appeared to be a chronic complainer. The problems she focused on were not even within the responsibilities of the executives she was conferring with. It is not surprising that her bad timing and her inability to respond directly to the firm's crises resulted in people feeling annoyed and even threatened by her activities. Janet was attempting to control her work environment—at the expense of others.

On the *emotional* level, neither her boss nor the other key members of the firm were in any condition to deal with future needs of the company. Keeping up with the daily crises was about all they could handle, when Janet was asking for their attention to proposals for the company's potential needs and her personal growth. Unwittingly, Janet set herself up to look like an empire builder. She had created a boomerang, mainly as a result of poor timing.

Here are some of the things you need to know to establish *positive* control over your work environment.

People function both on the emotional and rational levels. To illustrate: When someone bumps into you on the street, your first response is anger. Someone is deliberately trying to harm you! When the person apologizes, you realize that it was an accident and put the matter out of your mind.

Your first response to this event was *emotional*; your feelings told you that this was probably a hostile action, and you responded with hostility. Once you realized, with the rational part of your mind, that it wasn't a hostile action, you were able to give it the order of importance it deserved: none.

An alternative response might have been: You turn to the person and call him a name. He responds by hitting you. You then react by drawing a weapon and killing him. This is an extreme example, but the newspapers often report just such action-reaction events.

The importance of a balance between emotional and rational reactions to events cannot be overstated. Let's consider the role our emotions play in interpersonal relations: At the positive end of the spectrum, our feelings are the fuel that powers all our ideas and actions. Nothing can be achieved by any of us without involving our emotions. At the negative end, the uncontrolled force of the emotions leads to death and destruction.

One immediate deduction we can make from this is that emotions, *without the benefit of rational judg-*

ment, have no relative sense of weight—it's all or nothing, black or white, life or death. Often the first reaction to criticism is: "He hates me!" It has been said that at the purely emotional level, we are all four years old; when we become emotional, we automatically revert to childhood. All events in the world around us are seen as totally people related. So, in the grip of negative emotions, we tend to blame *people*, not analyze situations.

- "If I had a different boss, I'd love my job."
- "If management knew what they were doing, we'd be making twice the profits."
- "The reason I don't get promoted is because my boss is jealous of me."

When we function at the emotional level we feel powerless; we seem to have no control over events. Access to our rational mind helps us reestablish control.

We use our rational minds to modify our emotions. The rational mind packages, channels, and directs the raw force of emotional power. Maturity is measured by the dual skills of being able to use the rational part of our minds to channel our emotions, and to use the emotions to give positive force to our ideas, thoughts, and decisions.

To better understand the role the emotions play in your daily life, try to think of a positive emotional experience: praise or applause you received, for instance, for a job well done. Reexperience the event. What was your reaction? In what way did it influence any future actions? What was your subsequent relationship with the person or persons who praised you?

Donna J.'s experience illustrates a positive emotional chain of reactions. When Donna began work as executive secretary to the president of a real estate management business, she recognized that her boss spent a great deal of time responding to tenants' complaints. Donna was also aware that her boss didn't like this part of his job, yet he took pride in the company's reputation for responding to tenant problems quickly and courteously. Donna proposed that she could handle most calls herself, assuring him that she would respond in a way that would reflect the company's good-will policy.

Donna's boss welcomed the opportunity to get help with complaints, and praised her for taking the initiative to ask for more responsibility. This response from her boss gave Donna an immediate uplift and she felt doubly motivated to make good in her newly acquired task.

Looking back, Donna saw this as the beginning of a chain of events which led her to the position of office manager for the company. She now feels that she would be sure of acknowledgment and reward anytime she offered to solve a problem for her boss.

Now think of a negative emotional experience: unfair criticism or a situation perceived as unfair at the emotional level. Did this experience lead to a deterioration in your relationship with the other person? Or did you rationally "work it out" with him or her?

Martin K.'s case illustrates a purely emotional reaction which led to rapid deterioration of a relationship. He overheard one of the accountants he supervised say, "Martin isn't very effective at running this department, is he?" From that point on, every conversation Martin had with this subordinate was loaded with hostility. When he demanded, "Where are the cost-analysis reports you've been working on?" his subordinate replied, "You said you didn't need them until Tuesday." "You should have finished them already," Martin retorted. "I could have done them in two hours." The accountant threw the file on Martin's desk, said, "Then you do them!" and walked out of the office, slamming the door behind him.

Roslyn B., on the other hand, recognized a negative situation starting when she was asked repeatedly to get coffee for her boss. She reacted with hostility at first, but realized that if she continued to deal with the situation emotionally, she might ultimately get fired.

She asked to have a discussion with her boss about her job responsibilities and her role in the organization. She was surprised to discover that her boss was quite responsive and was actually embarrassed at what he referred to as his "unconscious male chauvinism."

These emotional trends, or action-reaction cycles, are a common feature of on-the-job relationships. Here are some examples:

Action: Robert S., director of public relations for a national service organization, received a memo from the president of the company. The memo included the following statement: "Please attach copies of your letters and all other applicable written material you generate to your monthly activity reports."

Reaction: "He doesn't even read my monthly reports! Why should I copy everything I do? It's a waste of time and an insult to my professionalism. Nobody at my level is expected to do this kind of reporting."

Result: Robert dutifully but grudgingly assembled the requested material for his report. To his surprise, he discovered great pleasure in presenting a rather impressive display of his activities. An even greater surprise was a subsequent memo from the president commending him on his work in general and the quality of his written materials in particular.

Action: Phil's proposal that his title of "Engineering Assistant" be changed to "Electronics Engineer" was rejected by his boss on the grounds that Phil did not have the appropriate college degree.

Reaction: "I do more sophisticated technical work than half the engineers in the company. This is a totally arbitrary and stupid decision. There's no way to get ahead here on the basis of real merit!"

Result: Phil's relationship with his boss became too tense for either of them to tolerate. Phil eventually saw the writing on the wall and left the company.

Action: As secretary to the operations manager of a radio station, Joyce contributed a number of ideas for feature programming. Her boss commended her on her creativity and said that she had considerable talent in this area.

Reaction: Joyce was eager to please her boss by fulfilling her regular secretarial duties and went further by making a number of formal proposals for feature programs.

Result: Within the year, Joyce was promoted to feature programming coordinator.

In each of these cases, emotional reactions had the potential to destroy or improve a relationship. In Robert's case, his rational mind kept him on the track with his boss long enough to create a new, positive emotional experience. Phil and Joyce responded emotionally. Lucky for Joyce, not so for Phil. In his case, there might have been a number of positive, rational approaches that could have improved his relationship with his boss and perhaps won him a promotion.

When you review, one by one, all the people in your work environment, you will find that your relationships with them are in a state of flux. In the long run, your relationships move in positive or negative directions, however static they may seem at a given moment. In some cases relationships cycle back and forth. In others they are definitely moving upwards or downwards. A positive emotional trend means that a positive action or statement by one partner in the relationship will generate a positive response, which in turn will bring about its own positive response, as in Donna J.'s experience in the real estate management firm. A negative emotional trend means the opposite, as in Martin K.'s case.

Your ideal goal will be to create an environment of 100 percent positive emotional trends in all your relationships. Note: We are not suggesting 100 percent positive relationships; you probably couldn't stand the ecstasy of it all! We are asking that you establish positive *trends*, in the direction of *improved* relationships, with all your coworkers and associates. It's a good direction to move in.

Begin with the relationships that are uncertain and are changing from day to day. One of the easiest starting points in creating a positive trend in a relationship is to smile at a person when he or she least expects it. It's irresistible—the other person can hardly keep from smiling back.

The next step is to turn around a negative emotional trend, where hostility has been met with hostility, or worse, noncommunication. Fortunately, there is a relatively easy way to do this also: Ignore the negative trend altogether. (Yes, even if you *owe* the other person an expletive, or at least a nasty sneer.) Start a positive trend by acknowledging a skill or talent in the other person or even asking his or her help in that area. Obviously, the request must be sincere. Tricks or ploys produce only short-lived results.

But putting all of a past troubled relationship on a shelf and starting a brand-new positive trend or relationship is not easy. It takes practice, so start by taking on a minor negative trend, not your arch enemy.

Henry T., for example, was a stockbroker in a prestigious firm. He was assigned a secretary, Linda, who also took calls, messages, and provided typing service to three other brokers. They were long-standing and politically influential members of the firm, while Henry was twenty four, just out of training, and considered an upstart. The trouble first began when he learned he wasn't getting his phone messages, and his clients had been treated curtly on the telephone. Soon he discovered that Linda considered his typing needs the lowest priority. He sometimes waited two days for simple letters to be completed. When he passed by Linda's desk on his way in and out of the office, she seemed to turn away, doing her best to ignore him.

Henry was angry! But he couldn't pin her attitude on anything he'd done, so he decided she was just a pain in the neck that he'd have to learn to live with. If she wasn't going to be decent enough to say hello, then why should *he*? He talked to her only out of necessity, and she followed suit.

More and more complaints came from clients who resented the way Linda treated them on the phone. Because the other brokers seemed to think she was a great secretary, Henry realized he wouldn't get support for his problem. He also knew that his success with a number of clients hinged on the way they were served. Henry had to turn the situation around.

He simply walked up to Linda's desk and said, "Hi, how are you today?" She responded with "Okay thanks." Not exactly her life story, but better than a cold silence. Henry continued to take the initiative at communicating and made a point of being polite but not overly solicitous. If they met by chance in the elevator, he'd make conversation like, "How's your four-year-old? I've always loved kids at that age." And he made sure to greet her with a genuine smile whenever he passed her desk.

He discovered that Linda couldn't help but respond positively. In fact she went as far as admitting that she resented it when she had been assigned to him, because none of the other secretaries had four bosses.

Helen G. offers another interesting case study. She had been asked to create a publicity event at the opening of her company's new manufacturing facility. She was told that the company's founder, although semiretired, would be the point of focus for the day. Helen decided that the founder's personal "American Dream" business story would be a good basis for promoting the event.

She had only one afternoon to prepare for the following morning's ribbon-cutting ceremony and reception for local dignitaries and members of the press. Helen had been looking forward to meeting the company's founder, but soon found him to be impossibly demanding. He insisted on having control over the entire event.

Helen felt if she responded to every question and demand he made, she'd have no time to run the event at all. He'd ask, "What are you saying to the reporters? Who are you calling? Where are you going? Who wrote this biography of me?" And he demanded, "This has to be rewritten. I want to know what you're doing. I won't come to the dedication if you can't tell me what's going on."

Helen had neither the time nor the patience at this point to apprise the man of each detail and to cater to his demands. Her relationship with him, however brief, progressed from pleasant to tense to impossible in one afternoon. The following day's dedication went smoothly but left Helen feeling angry and hoping she'd never have to put up with him again.

After this event, she made every attempt to be scarce whenever the firm's founder was on the premises. After a few such incidents, she realized the situation was getting ridiculous. She decided to make a real effort to start communicating positively with him.

To her surprise, he seemed willing to make a fresh start and never mentioned their previous encounter. Mutual interest in the company was now the basis for all their communication.

The founder would tell Helen long stories about how he started the business and built it up, and she found herself responding with genuine interest.

For both Helen and Henry, the willingness to take the initiative helped turn a negative emotional trend into a positive one.

In order to understand emotional trends, look at their points of origin. There is good evidence for the fact that people rarely do anything for you or against you in the *first instance*. As an example: I may give you a raise, or not give you a raise in order to suit my budget. Your response and reaction to my decision helps to determine our future relationship. If I give you a raise and your gratitude results in a positive attitude and effort, I'll probably give you a bigger raise next time.

If, on the other hand, I decide I can't afford to give you a raise, and your reaction is hostility and noncooperation, I may eventually fire you. In this case my original action may have been caused merely by my own financial condition and not by any fault of yours. But my action, together with your reaction, started a negative emotional trend, ending in a loss for both of us.

The rational response for you would be to nip the negative trend in the bud by demonstrating your value positively.

For example, Jack B. was in line for his yearly review and, according to his own assessment of his work, due for a raise. He had started his operations management position with a small but expanding manufacturing firm about a year before. At that time, the company was only six months old and had no formal production schedules or quality maintenance systems. He developed and implemented both, often working late at night. He believed his boss appreciated and recognized the value of his contribution.

Jack wrote a memo to his boss, mentioning the length of time Jack had been on the job and referring to some of his contributions. He requested a meeting to discuss his salary.

Jack was surprised and shocked when he received a memo from his boss: "There will be no salary adjustments at this time." He was further confounded and hurt by the impersonal nature of the communication.

The following day, Jack approached his boss and asked for a brief meeting. By this time, Jack had cooled down, considered his options, and decided on a course of action. He asked his boss, "Are there problems in the company that I could help with? Your memo seemed to indicate a new condition I wasn't aware of."

Much to his relief, Jack was told that the firm was in the midst of making a large investment. His boss, in turn, was relieved that Jack didn't press the salary review. The boss expressed his appreciation for the way Jack handled the matter and suggested they talk again in two months about a salary review.

As you know, of all working relationships, the one with your boss is the most sensitive and complicated. Once you master that, dealing with your peers and subordinates will be easy by comparison.

At the purely emotional level, we blame people rather than evaluating situations. So, our tendency is to personify our job. We make people—our boss or others—responsible for everything that happens in our job. Because moving from the emotional to the rational level would mean taking responsibility when we'd prefer not to, we are often content to give our feelings free reign and blame others for our condition. A whole body of code language regarding "bosses" has become established among employees at every level.

Common Expressions: Emotionally Motivated Code Language	They Usually Mean
My boss is dishonest!	The reality of my job turned out to be different from what my boss

Common Expressions: Emotionally Motivated Code Language	They Usually Mean
	and I discussed when I was hired. Promises haven't been kept. My perceptions are different from my boss's.
My boss is incompetent!	I'm not given credit for the superior skills *I* have.
My boss is a crook!	My standards are superior to my boss's. His goals aren't in line with mine.
I don't think my boss likes me!	I haven't really communicated with my boss in months

The statements on the left are expressions of feeling. Most of the time they are simple, black or white emotional platforms on which to rest your case and your mind. They are attractive simplifications because they eliminate the responsibility for action. But they also lead to negative trends in boss relationships and, eventually, complete communications breakdowns and job severance.

The statements on the right are more rational descriptions of the problems involved and are capable of being dealt with. Job descriptions can be changed, promises can be retrieved, skills can be acknowledged, communications can be reestablished, and even superior standards can be expressed and implemented without a breakdown in boss/subordinate relationships.

Whenever you find yourself making a simple statement about your boss or any other people you work with, examine it carefully. You may be using code language describing a feeling rather than a fact. One clue to this is that at the emotional level, you will tend to personify problems. As we've shown earlier, you'll tend to blame people rather than describing actual problems or situations.

In order to function positively in a people environment, you can get out of a negative emotional trap by using your rational mind to identify and solve the actual problem.

Tony E. started out liking his computer programming job and feeling that his boss was a creative programmer, likable, and supportive of his staff. About a year after he started, Tony noticed how little he got to talk to his boss. It seemed that his boss didn't want to talk to any of the staff members, avoided making new assignments, and practically hid in his office to avoid confrontations. Tony was unable to reach him to get approval for projects they had talked about implementing months before.

Furthermore, he was pretty certain there was something strange going on in the company or in his department. Why else would his boss be so reclusive?

Tony decided that his boss was an incompetent manager, and probably dishonest as well.

Feeling that there would be no chance for advancement with this kind of boss, Tony found each day on the job just more drudgery. His suspicions about his boss made him feel uncomfortable in all of their communications, and the relationship became even more tense.

Tony considered looking for a new job but wasn't thrilled about the idea of hitting the pavement again. One day another programmer in his department mentioned how depressed their boss was and hinted that he had some really serious problems. It suddenly dawned on Tony that he might have made a wrong conclusion about his boss's behavior and the motivations behind it. Remembering the really good rapport they'd had in the past, Tony decided to take a shot at finding out what was going on.

Tony arrived at work an hour early the next day, sure that his boss would already be there. He found him working on a program in the main computer room. He offered his boss a cup of coffee and soon found himself talking as easily as he'd done months ago. Tony was surprised when his boss revealed that he was unhappy with his job, disliked all of the "administrative nonsense" he had to deal with, and wished he could do some really creative programming again. He confessed that he felt so trapped and depressed that he talked to as few people as possible.

Tony now had the facts. The reality of his work situation was a far cry from his perceptions. His negative emotional reaction to that perceived reality might have resulted in quitting, or being fired as a result of an increasingly tense relationship with his boss.

Instead, Tony was able to reverse this emotional condition and to propose solutions that would benefit his boss as well as his own ambitions. As a result, Tony willingly took on some of the tasks his boss found irritating, gained greater responsibility, and simultaneously increased his value to the company.

We did say that the emotions can be both positive and negative. Suppose you find yourself saying: My boss is great! This may be emotional code language for: I enjoy my job. I'm doing what I want to do. I'm in tune with my boss!

Wonderful! Enjoy the feeling. Remember that it is reinforced by the quality of the work you do in such a situation. Continue to be productive and, at the same time, nurture the good relationship with your boss.

Even great relationships on the job need daily care and feeding. Your ability to establish and maintain all those relationships depends on your understanding of the role the emotions play in interpersonal communications, and on your skill in balancing your emotions with rational thoughts and actions.

On the other hand, sometimes escape from a heavily charged emotional situation may seem impossible, for example, if you did not get a promotion or are having a fight with a boss or associate. The oldest solution is still the best: TIME.

Don't try to be "rational" about the problem right away. The heavier the emotional charge, the longer it takes to discharge it. Allow several hours or even days to pass without forcing yourself to cope with your feelings.

But be careful not to take any action during that time so you don't set off a negative action-response cycle that you won't be able to control. And make sure you resolve to review the event in the light of your rational mind at some point, in order to remove any emotional blocks that may get in your way later.

Jeff C., for example, was the design engineer for a new piece of computer equipment his company was showing to a prospective customer. A series of problems had shown up in the design the day before, and Jeff felt the sales pitch was being made prematurely.

The sales manager, Rick (a trained engineer), was demonstrating the item to the customer and couldn't get it to work. Looking on, Jeff realized he had a solution. He offered his help, but Rick just snapped back, "That won't work. I don't need my time being wasted right now."

Although he was seething and feeling humiliated, Jeff quietly left the scene. He didn't want to create an even worse situation in front of the customer. He knew that if he said anything, it would reflect his true sentiments. And his feelings at the moment were that Rick was an incompetent jerk.

That night, Jeff told his wife what had happened. She was surprised, because Jeff had previously told her how professional Rick was.

Jeff decided to wait and see if Rick would take action

toward a resolution. He remembered how well they had worked together for the past year and realized that things might be easier to resolve once the pressure was off.

Late the next afternoon, Rick approached Jeff and apologized for what had happened. Jeff was able to discuss the situation in terms of their mutual professional goals, rather than in terms of a negative emotional reaction to the event.

It helps to understand the role feelings play in our work life, if we realize that, emotionally, all of us are in the center of our own universe. This means that all our actions must be acceptable to ourselves. If they aren't, we'll make them so.

To illustrate this phenomenon, let's use our previous example of giving or withholding a salary increase. Assume I don't give you an increase even though you feel you've earned one. As you remember, I didn't give it to you because I felt I couldn't afford it. I now have to make this action acceptable to myself. I suddenly remember that you were late for work twice during the last month, and once—horrors—you didn't say good morning. *Of course* you didn't deserve a raise.

You now pick up these waves of negative feelings caused by my need to validate my decision. You retaliate by coming in late every morning and by eliminating greetings altogether. You have now helped me to justify my salary decision. Next time around I certainly won't give you a raise and soon after that, I'll probably fire you.

Now let's turn from this gloomy example to its opposite. I decide, in spite of my tight budget, to give you a salary increase. Was this a prudent thing to do? I don't know, so I'll get busy validating: I remember that you worked late into the evening one day last week. That certainly proves that you deserved a raise (!). You'll again retaliate in the positive sense, by working extra hard and giving me a nice smile every morning. I now feel my decision of giving you an increase was one of my better investments.

The foregoing is, of course, a caricature, and it is somewhat simplified for purposes of easy communication, but not much. The dynamics involved are accurately described. The logical conclusion is that you can't afford to be passed over for a raise when you feel one is due you. By pressing for an increase, however small (using the methods described in the following chapters), you will set in motion a positive validating process in the mind of your boss.

People who have followed this advice have received better-than-average salary increases for at least three years following the event, even without taking any further action.

It should go without saying that your skills and talents must be suited to the job you're doing. At the same time, you need to be *emotionally* in tune with your job. In other words, your values and purposes must be in tune with those of your employers (see chapter 3).

"That's a tall order. How can I possibly know what my employer's purposes are?" The answer is: Ask!

The challenge is that while the overall goal of an organization may be relatively constant, short-range goals, problems, opportunities, and the approaches to dealing with them change almost every day. To be aware of all of them, and to be emotionally in tune with them, could be a full-time task, allowing no time or energy for doing anything else in your job. But without this awareness, true involvement in your job and real job fulfillment are not possible.

Now that you are armed with sound principles for building constructive relationships on the job, you are ready to make a specific plan of action.

CHAPTER 7

THE IN-COMPANY CAMPAIGN: A BASIC RECIPE FOR MANAGING YOUR JOB

You are now ready to design your strategy to bring about a change in your job or job environment. Bringing about such a change is called an *In-company Campaign*. "In-company" refers to the fact that it takes place on the job, within the limits of the organization that employs you. "Campaign" implies that there is an objective to be achieved, as in an advertising or election campaign, where the *result* is the rationale for and an integral part of the whole.

"But," you may be saying, "isn't a campaign a very complex undertaking? I'm not sure I'm ready for such a step. Besides, I've already tried to improve my work situation, but I got nowhere."

This last sentence may contain the answer to the first two. Before we respond in more detail, see if the following quotes sound familiar to you:

- "Lately all my proposals have been ignored. No one seems to pay any attention to me."

- "I haven't had a real salary increase in three years."
- "I'm just being used by my employer."
- "Company policy keeps me from doing things the way I think they should be done."
- "I hate my job."
- "I'm being discriminated against because . . ."

We, and people like us, often react to such statements with: "Well, why don't you do something about your situation?" Specific suggestions along the lines of mounting an organized campaign to deal with the problem are usually met with another set of familiar responses:

- "I think I'll just look for another job."
- "You don't know my boss—it wouldn't do any good to do anything."
- "I'm not aggressive enough to argue with my employer."
- "I'll just have to learn to live with the problem."
- "In my company the only way to get ahead is to conform."
- "The only way to get around the problem is to use dirty tricks. I'm not that kind of person."

The most frequently heard objections to on-the-job problem solving using an In-company Campaign are that it sounds too complicated and seems too risky, in terms of "putting one's head on the block."

Conducting an In-company Campaign, in fact, is simple because it is based on common sense. It's safe because the method is founded on the principles of constructive human relations. Tens of thousands of people have done it with great success, sometimes under the guidance and supervision of professional career counselors.

The In-company Campaign is also an ideal response to the following type of question:

- "I'm ready for a more responsible position; how do I go about getting it?"
- "I've just finished a project. I feel I've done a good job. My boss does too. How can I best capitalize on this to get a promotion?"
- "I heard that there's going to be an opening in the ————department. This could be my big opportunity. Whom do I talk to about this?"

The third area in which to apply the In-company Campaign concept is job burnout. This is a condition brought about by a mismatch between a person's motivated skills and talents, and the requirements of his or her job. Heavy workload, uncongenial environment, and low pay frequently trigger burnout but are not the underlying cause of it.

Whether you want to solve a problem, take advantage of an opportunity, or create an opportunity, the In-company Campaign is a safe, effective way to do it. It isn't a method for lodging a protest or complaint. The In-company Campaign is a procedure for *mobilizing the best resources* available to you to bring about a change or adjustment in your work or your job that measurably *increases your level of job satisfaction*. Liking your work more is accompanied by higher productivity, which accounts for the high success record of the method you're about to learn.

But there are a few ground rules, as you've seen from reading the preceding chapters. We'll review these here:

Ground Rule No. 1: Before starting an In-company Campaign, make sure your work is up to the standard your employer expects. No one will listen to you or be interested in doing anything for you if your work is behind schedule or below standard.

Ground Rule No. 2: Make all reasonable efforts to have a positive day-to-day working relationship with your superiors and others. If there is an open break or conflict with any person in your immediate working environment, correct it. It's best to set a time limit (one or two months) and work at starting a positive emotional trend (see chapter 5). If that isn't done, an In-company Campaign is no longer safe. It's important to "protect your rear" in any forward move. It won't help if someone in your immediate vicinity is looking for an excuse to do you in!

Ground Rule No. 3: Avoid short-order cooking. The method here described is simple, but it *only* works if you follow it *all the way.*

Certainly there have been instances where a simple chat with the boss has produced spectacular results, just as there are winners in many games of chance. Some even like the challenge of the roulette wheel. But here we are talking about a professional approach to job and career growth and not about a game.

There are four steps in an In-company Campaign:

STEP I.   SETTING YOUR OBJECTIVE
STEP II. PREPARING YOUR PRESENTATION
STEP III. MAKING YOUR PRESENTATION
STEP IV. FOLLOW-THROUGH TO RESULT

That's all there is to it! We'll show you in detail how to manage each of the four steps:

STEP I. *SETTING YOUR OBJECTIVE*
Your objective may be to get an extra light fixture installed to save your eyesight, a salary increase, a vice-presidency, or any of a hundred different adjustments or advances in your work situation. But all objectives

will have one thing in common: They will benefit both you *and* your employer!

Therefore, an integral part of the objective-setting process is the research necessary to determine how your purpose fits into the framework of the total organization. Make sure you have an up-to-date organizational chart and a description of your key associates to refer to (see chapter 3). This also is where your Contact/Information Network comes into its own. Key members of your C/I Network can also be used to help you make sure your objective is realistic, through informal, off-the-record discussions.

Otherwise you may find yourself setting an objective or making a proposal that is based on a wrong assumption or is out of tune with the purposes of your employers. You might well make a flawless case for it by writing down impressive past credentials and genuine intentions of future contributions. But it still won't fly. Emotionally we tend to superimpose our own desires on reality. We can prove almost any point we wish to make. To ourselves!

Arnold S. supported his objective of advancing to a senior marketing position for a chain of optical stores by making a number of proposals to the company's president. Carefully outlining the needs of customers and citing expertise available within the company, he demonstrated the potential benefit of introducing a number of new product lines, such as contact lenses, binoculars, etc.

Arnold's credentials and experience with the company supported his objective beautifully, but he was turned down for the position he requested.

The problem was that what looked like a great plan to Arnold was completely out of tune with the current goals of the company. For better or worse, the president's purpose at that point was to expand the company's territory, not its range of products.

It's admittedly difficult to strike the exact balance between benefiting your employer and benefiting yourself equally, when considering your objective. But it's not too difficult to avoid extremes in either direction.

Another consideration is the relative magnitude of your objective. As a rule of thumb, start by setting relatively easy objectives, such as adding one or two duties to your job description or getting a change in your title. Once you have practice in conducting an In-company Campaign, you can tackle bigger objectives. Whenever you plan to ask for a major change in your work situation, especially one that would involve a change in the company's structure as well, you should consider dividing your objective into two or more parts and taking them one step at a time.

Roger B.'s case illustrates this technique. As sales manager for a retail clothing chain, he aspired to be the director of marketing for the company. No one had actually had such a position before, so he would have to create the job himself. A further difficulty in achieving this objective was the fact that he had never communicated his business and marketing capabilities directly to the president of the company.

Roger's first step was to create a regular vehicle for communication between himself and the president. Roger did this by issuing a bimonthly sales report to the president, in which he included his marketing ideas and specific proposals to implement them. He followed each memo with a telephone call or a request to meet with the president. Roger used these occasions to communicate his business know-how and to get feedback on his marketing ideas.

After six or seven months, Roger realized that his relationship with the president had taken an entirely new turn. The reception he had gotten for his ideas and his actual accomplishments in his job made the time right for his next step: a proposal to be made director of marketing.

This brings up a question that is often asked: Should you reserve the In-company Campaign methodology for major, complex changes in your work structure? The answer is an emphatic NO. The whole point of an In-company Campaign is that it is based on common sense and the way people normally function. There is no better way to solve on-the-job problems and bring about on-the-job changes, whatever the size of the problems or changes involved.

What is equally common sense is to tailor the size of the effort to the size of the objective. It would be fatuous to write a seven-page presentation to get a light bulb changed, just as it would be inept to expect a short, handwritten note to bring about a major reorganization of a multimillion dollar company. The following examples illustrate this point.

Laura F. was a production assistant at a small television station. In order to perform her job successfully, a good rapport with her show's technical director was essential. Unfortunately, the technical director didn't take her very seriously, and dismissed as unimportant all the instructions that she relayed from her boss, the executive producer of the show. Her boss resented this, of course, so Laura and the technical director were heading for a personality collision.

This was clearly not a situation that required a major effort, accompanied by a ten-page proposal. Laura's objective was simply to start a step-by-step process to improve her relationship and to reverse the negative emotional trend between herself and the technical director, or she stood a good chance of losing her job.

On the other hand, Joe G.'s situation, at the same television station, presented a more complicated problem. As general manager for the station, he was becoming increasingly anxious about the reduction in advertising revenues. Joe felt a major sales campaign would be necessary to attract new sponsors and get back some of the old ones. He had the selling expertise and enough manpower, but as far as he was concerned, not enough control over the product. What Joe wanted to do was to have a stronger hand in the programming decisions for the station. This would require a decision from the board of directors, and a general realignment of responsibilities in the upper management of the station.

Joe's case is a good example of the need for a more complex and sophisticated In-company Campaign plan.

For more detailed information on setting objectives, review chapter 3. To be absolutely sure that your objective makes sense, move to the next step.

STEP II. *PREPARING YOUR PRESENTATION*
Once you've set an objective for yourself, you need to communicate it to the right person in order to implement it. What is the best way to do this?

There are two schools of thought. One holds that oral communications are best because they are direct, personal, and allow you to employ the full range of your personality, salesmanship, and emotional power. The other school of thought is that a written presentation has the advantage of greater logic, can be honed to a fine edge before it is submitted, is more professional because of the trouble taken to prepare it, and has greater staying power because of its relative permanency.

Both views are correct. So you'll be using a combination of both approaches.

Let's analyze these two forms of communication further.

WRITTEN PRESENTATION

Advantages	*Disadvantages*
• It presents your point of view clearly structured and focused with no distractions in presenting a logical case.	• It is an indirect form of communication and therefore, of necessity, impersonal.
• All points can be presented positively without negative emotions clouding the issue.	• It does not allow you to show your positive feelings about an issue, except in an abstract way.
• It will serve as an agenda for purposeful, face-to-face discussion.	• It is sometimes said that written material isn't safe because it can fall into the wrong hands. (We'll show the importance of keeping your presentations entirely positive.)
• Aids memory and follow-through. (It won't go away until it has been acted upon.)	

ORAL PRESENTATION

Advantages	*Disadvantages*
• It enables you to communicate your feelings directly, accurately, and powerfully.	• It has no permanence, (Often it's "in one ear and out the other.")
• It's the best way to persuade or convince someone, and to make the "sale."	• Few people remember discussions accurately.
• It allows you to see the other person's response, and to deal with it constructively.	• It forces you to make too many ad-hoc decisions; you may be tempted to "make it up as you go along."
	• There's the danger of letting negative feelings about past events show and get in the way of constructive communication.

We trust we have made our point and convinced you to combine the advantages of both written and oral presentations whenever it's possible. When you use a combination, the disadvantages of both will cancel each other out.

For detailed instructions of how to prepare an effective written presentation, see chapter 8.

STEP III. *MAKING YOUR PRESENTATION*

There are two ways to be sure that you're ready for Step III. Reread your presentation twenty-four hours after you have written the first draft. See if it still makes sense, states your points clearly, and, above all, demonstrates a positive attitude. Also, if possible, show it to a member of your C/I Network who is in a position to evaluate it objectively. (You don't necessarily have to follow his or her advice, but you should consider it.)

Timing is important in making a presentation to superiors. Asking for a substantial salary increase on the very day your company lost a major contract is a classic example of bad timing.

Timing of your presentation also avoids off-the-cuff emotional responses. Once someone says no to you, it's very difficult for that person to reverse him or herself. Yet the initial emotional *no* may have been caused simply by a momentary sense of inconvenience or a misunderstanding of your intentions, when the recipient is under time pressure.

There is also the problem of not being aware of your boss's state of mind at any given moment. Organizational problems, financial problems, or a specific task your boss has been asked to perform in a hurry could be a barrier to a positive consideration of your proposal.

We have found that the best time to convey the written presentation to a superior is at the end of a work day, or even better, a work week. As you'll remember, the rational mind needs time to get control of the emotions. Because you are making a rational, well-thought-out case, you are appealing to the rational faculties of the recipient and will have to give him or her time to digest the material.

> Marketing Vice-President George K., for example, presented a proposal for an increase in his advertising budget at a time when his manufacturing firm was in deep financial trouble. The proposal would no doubt create emotional waves, but his presentation contained a carefully written program for advertising expenditures which would be likely to increase sales before the bills would have to be paid, and so ultimately reduce the company's debt.
> George knew that just an oral request for more money would be turned down flat. The written proposal would give his boss time to get to the solutions before he answered purely on the basis of his emotions.

Once again we want to reemphasize the importance of combining written and oral presentations. The temptation to shortcut the process can be great. Most people have fairly informal relationships with their superiors. The authors have frequently heard questions like "Isn't it silly to write a letter to someone I talk with all the time?" No, it isn't! The less formal your usual relationship with a person, the more important it is to demonstrate your seriousness and determination by choosing an unusual or different method of communication.

For a more detailed description of this third step in your In-company Campaign, see chapter 9.

STEP IV. *FOLLOW-THROUGH TO RESULT*
One of the positive aspects of the In-company Campaign methodology is that *there is always a next step.*

As long as you proceed along the lines we have outlined, you'll always be perceived as constructive, positive, alive, growing, cooperative, and responsible.

Even after you've achieved your immediate objective, you'll continue to benefit from the positive trend
you've helped to start and the momentum of your forward motion. But a certain level of energy is needed
to keep your In-company Campaign moving, because
there is a danger in discontinuing it. People will conclude that you weren't serious in the first place, that
you didn't "mean it." And they'll take you less seriously if you ask for anything again in the future.

Therefore, *follow-up is the most crucial part of the
In-company Campaign.* You'll get help in doing this
when you read chapter 10.

The following is a brief summary of the basic recipe
for bringing about a change in your job or job environment; in short, a way to take control of and manage
your job.

Preparation: • Bring your job up-to-date and up-to-
standard.
• Review your working relationships
with the key people in your organization, and take time to convert any negative trends into positive ones.
• Draw an organizational diagram of
your company, including *realistic* reporting lines.
• Write down brief descriptions of your
key associates who would most likely be
involved in any move you make, or be
affected by it.

In-company Campaign: • Set your objective
• Prepare your presentation
• Make your presentation
• Follow-through to result.

We suggest using a bookmark to enable you to find this page easily. You'll need to refer to these points frequently, at least until you have made them a habit.

Now let's see if the next-step objective you've set for yourself still makes sense when it's documented in stark black and white.

CHAPTER 8

THE WRITTEN PRESENTATION: DOCUMENTING YOUR FUTURE

How can you document your future? And what's the point of documenting your past?

The best answer responds to both questions at the same time: You document future potential by documenting past achievements. A written presentation is the most effective way to document anything. But as we've seen in the last chapter, it's an unreliable vehicle for conveying your feelings. So it must be followed by a face-to-face meeting to complete the process of communication.

A written presentation to document a request for a promotion might start like this:

> "I respectfully request a meeting to review the following contributions I've made to the company over the past six months . . ."

The presentation, of course, may go on to list the writer's contributions and accomplishments, but probably will convey little of the enthusiasm and loyalty that motivated each item in the presentation.

On the other hand, a request for a promotion during a face-to-face meeting with your boss, during which you can show your enthusiasm for your work and your employer, may not get you much more than a smile and a pat on the back. Experience shows that such requests evaporate into thin air shortly after the event. Most decision makers are too busy to remember such verbal presentations for more than a few hours. Even though your boss may agree that your request certainly deserves consideration, action is usually long in coming—if ever.

The most powerful and productive way to get results, as we've said, is a combination of written and spoken communications. Our experience in helping thousands of people manage their jobs shows that this dual communications path brings consistent success in conducting an In-company Campaign.

So, if you want to get your point across and get action, make your case in writing; then follow through in person using the power of positive feelings to make the sale. Let's illustrate this with an example:

Earl K. wanted to improve communications with his boss. His objective was to set up weekly meetings to make sure he was in tune with his boss. Earl's first attempt at setting up the process was during an informal chat with his boss. Earl felt he had sufficiently good rapport to do this verbally.

Within three weeks the system was failing. Although Earl's boss had agreed wholeheartedly to the *idea* of the meetings, he turned out not to be available on most of the mornings they had agreed to meet.

Earl now realized that his verbal proposal, although received with enthusiasm, was not taken very seriously. His next step was a memo to his boss in which he formally requested regular meetings, clearly stated his purpose for the meetings, and finally suggested a first meeting to determine a mutually convenient, regular schedule. Earl discovered that his boss was surprised at the seriousness with which Earl viewed these meetings. He called Earl into his office, and after a brief discussion about purposes, agreed to a meeting schedule. This time the meetings did take place and resulted in improved rapport between Earl and his boss.

An even simpler, everyday use of the combination of written and spoken communications is Louis G.'s memo to his boss:

"This is just a reminder that I'll be out of the office tomorrow afternoon, as we discussed. If you need anything, Scott will be handling office affairs and can reach me for emergencies."

Providing your boss with a written reminder and assurance that you are aware of his or her needs can make the difference between a sound and positive working relationship, versus confusion and negative communication.

A more complex application of this method is Anthony C.'s In-company Campaign to obtain a change in his job title. After four years with the firm, his job function had gradually changed from technician's work to more complex engineering tasks, but his job title had remained "Technician." Over the years Anthony had become aware that the head of his department had a tendency to ignore, or respond negatively to, memos or any other written notes. However, Anthony was very much in earnest about upgrading his title and the recognition he felt was due him. He decided that only a written proposal could properly document his case. On the other hand, Anthony realized that in order for his boss to understand his goal on a positive emotional level, and to respond with action, a verbal presentation was essential as well. While making his presentation in his boss's office, Anthony expressed his appreciation for the opportunity to learn on the job and attributed much of his career progress to the help he had received from his boss. Anthony's combined presentations conveyed the correct proportions of serious intent and positive attitude to achieve his goal.

You may ask why we are making such heavy weather over the relatively simple issue of writing notes to your boss. And why do we use such a seemingly pompous term as "presentation" when describing a letter or memo?

The answer to the first question is that only by dramatizing this technique can we hope to convince you that something so simple can be so important. How often have you asked for something, big or small, and been turned down? The easy extra step of putting your requests on paper will often make the difference between being ignored and being taken seriously. We are not suggesting that you stop talking with people and start communicating by way of written notes. We *are* saying that written notes or memos either precede or accompany any oral requests or proposals you make to your superiors.

As to "presentation," the slightly pompous aura of the word is intentional. It implies a certain amount of "ceremony"—something out of the ordinary—the exact opposite of "on the spur of the moment." Your intention is to *present* a well-thought-out plan.

There *are* exceptions to the above emphasis on written communications. *When the objective* to be achieved is a very minor one, *and* you're reasonably sure that the answer is yes, an informal verbal request may be perfectly sufficient.

For instance, Joel C. had already received a general okay from his boss to move into a larger office, but hadn't set up the timing to make the move. As soon as he had determined when the new space would be available, he simply asked his boss, "Is it all right with you if I move into my new office next Wednesday?"

Another case when a face-to-face conversation precedes a written presentation occurs when you want to informally "test the waters" for the correct timing to the formal presentation.

Michael H. was concerned about the decrease in sales at the discount clothing outlet he managed. He suggested to the owner, "I think we need a new ad campaign. I'd like to work with the agency on a new approach." His boss responded, "Good idea. Why don't you work out a budget?"

This was an invitation for Michael to make a formal presentation. On the other hand, had his boss said, "We haven't got a cent to spend on more advertising right now," Michael would have known that the timing was off for such a presentation.

Keep in mind that we are referring in this chapter to a presentation of facts designed to motivate your *superiors* to help you bring about a change in the status quo of your work situation. We are not suggesting that you conduct your normal everyday communications with your associates in writing.

In this chapter, then, we are describing the *written* presentation as part of an In-company Campaign. Chapter 10 will detail its verbal counterpart.

In order to formulate a convincing case, you need to tailor your presentation to the recipient. Every communication requires a sender and a receiver. One without the other is useless, for they are both part of the communications process. And they must both be on the same wavelength. The more you know about and are concerned with the reader, the more certain you can be of being heard, understood, and getting an appropriate response.

Depending on your personal style, the form of your usage could range all the way from "Hi—thought I'd put some of my thoughts on paper . . ." to "Dear Dr. Terwilliger: In view of our excellent past relationship . . .". When in doubt, stay on the formal side! And, yes, your presentation should always be typed. It's a courtesy to the reader and shows, once again, that you mean business.

A frequently asked question has been: "Aren't there times when a written communication can backfire?" Certainly! Here's a good example, or rather a bad one:

"Dear George,
   "The request you made of me to handle the matter we discussed yesterday is unfair and unethical. I feel I should not be put in this position."

The writer of this note was condemning his boss "without a trial." This is a case where a face-to-face discussion would have been a better way to get the facts and avoid starting a negative emotional trend.

Let's agree on the two ground rules: Any written communication, from a simple note to an elaborate proposal, must be totally constructive (not always easy to do), and must be tailored to the recipient. That means in tune with his or her personality, language, mood, and circumstances at the time of writing. If you don't know, ask a few questions and find out! (Remember your C/I Network.) Here's an example:

Carlos T. was the production manager for an eyeglass frame manufacturing plant. The president of the company visited the production facility only one day each month. Outside of that, Carlos had to communicate with him by mail or telephone at the home office, 150 miles away.

Production speed and efficiency needed improvement if Carlos were to meet the schedule he'd been given. He felt he could accomplish this by redesigning the interior space of the plant and adding a new piece of equipment. This would require getting a budget and his design ideas approved by the company president.

Carlos knew that a concise written proposal, without much detail, was what the president would best respond to. But since Carlos only saw him once a month, he was unaware of his boss's current mood, especially about spending money. So Carlos called a member of his C/I Network at the home office to find out. His contact told him that the president was going to be asked for a number of expense approvals from the departments within a couple of weeks. He suggested that Carlos make his proposal quickly. Carlos sent his written presentation immediately, called his boss to follow-up two days later, and got approval without argument.

Now, the $64,000 question in any In-company Campaign: To whom should you address your presentation? Another of our rules of thumb: Always write to the person who has the power to make a decision about your request or proposal.

In most cases that person will be your immediate superior. But not always. It may be a person more highly placed in the corporate hierarchy, or it may be the president or chairman of the board. In some instances it may be more than one person—in the case of a transfer both your boss and the head of the department to which you want to transfer are involved.

In some cases you may feel that your immediate boss may actually get in the way of what you're trying to achieve. For instance:

Ellen B., a research assistant for a large camera manufacturing company, was responsible for writing all of the product-performance reports that her boss presented to the company's board of directors, though he never mentioned Ellen's part in them. It was clear to Ellen that her boss's success record was based partly on her own work.

Ellen's In-company Campaign goal was, understandably, to transfer to another department in the company, where her research and reporting skills would be more valued, and where her accomplishments would be recognized as her own. She felt that her boss had too large a stake in having her remain on his staff, and determined that her presentation would be more successful if made to her boss's superior. On the other hand, she didn't really want to create a personality conflict with her current boss.

Whatever your situation, *your direct superior must never be left out of the process*. These are your options:

1. Go to your boss and say that you want to make a proposal to someone else (his or her boss, etc.), but that, naturally, you wouldn't go behind his or her back and would like permission to present your case to the other person. Your boss will react in one of the following ways:
   a) "Very well, you have my permission."
   b) "Tell me more about what you are trying to do. Then we'll see. . . ."
   c) "Now that you've told me more about what you want to propose, why don't you let me handle it for you."
   d) "I don't think this is a reasonable request. I suggest you forget it."

Your response to c) should be something like this:

"I don't want to burden you with what is really my responsibility. I'll follow through on this myself, but I *did* want to have your permission." (The implication is that you *will* follow through one way or the other, but you want to observe the amenities.)

The appropriate response to d) is:

"I don't want to pursue this without your permission, but I'm serious about it, and would be interested to know why you don't think it's a good idea." (Your boss may have valuable information that you hadn't considered. You may want to use it to rewrite your presentation.)

In our experience, no boss will risk a complete breakdown of his or her relationship with you unless it is already heavily strained, in which case you need to take time to rebuild it (Ground Rule #2, chapter 3).

Even if you decide to change your presentation or your timing in view of important new information, don't give up your intention of presenting your case to the final decision maker. If you see your immediate boss as a great obstacle to your In-company Campaign, make a dual presentation. Send the original of your presentation to the top decision maker, with a copy to your immediate superior, or address the presentation jointly to both. That will prevent your boss from scuttling your efforts. But remember, *having* to use this technique may mean that you should take a little time to rebuild your relationship with your boss before proceeding with your In-company Campaign.

It's not always easy to put important thoughts on paper. Don't try to write your proposal in one go-round—at least not until you've had lots of practice. Start by jotting down what you think you want to say on a piece of paper without regard to grammar, punctuation, or polish.

Read it over to see if it makes sense, correct it, rewrite portions of it, or change the sequence of the points you want to make until it starts to look good to you. Then copy it over and read it to someone else. You may be too close to the subject to see it clearly.

Now let your draft sit for a few hours or overnight. If it still makes sense, do your final typing or have it typed.

Only rarely is a memorandum format suitable for an In-company Campaign presentation. Memos tend to be impersonal, and most people get far too many of them to have any enthusiasm for reading another one.

Instead of: TO:_____
              FROM:_____
              SUBJECT:_____

use a normal letter format starting with Dear_____.

We have frequently been told that our insistence on the letter format flies in the face of traditional in-company communications practices.

Years of experience have convinced us that the letter format works better exactly because it is a departure from the normal, day-to-day practices in most organizations. It is both less common and more personal than the standard memo format. You'll see, just below, how any negative reactions are nipped in the bud by the opening paragraph of the letter.

Remember: You are asking for the recipient's personal consideration of your presentation, based on its merits, rather than the application of standard company policy.

We'll give you a paragraph-by-paragraph outline of what an In-company Campaign proposal or presentation should contain. You may then use your own words, and couch them in the style you believe would be most appropriate under the circumstances. If in doubt, it's better to err on the formal side rather than the informal. However, formal doesn't mean impersonal:

- Informal: I really got a boot out of kicking around the old place for the last four years. We've had a lot of laughs.

- Impersonal: I joined this firm on Jan. 4th, 1979. My work has been interesting.
- Formal: It's really been a pleasure working with you these four years. I've learned a lot during this time.

As you can see, formality does not exclude warmth. Here now is the outline of what an In-company Campaign presentation should contain and the reasons for it.

FIRST PARAGRAPH: DECLARATION OF LOYALTY

A person's first reaction to getting a letter from an employee, *before reading it*, is either "He's probably resigning," or "He must be complaining about something." At best, such a letter is an interruption of the work flow, and implies extra time spent on a possible problem. Your very first words must dispel that negative expectation and set a positive emotional climate. Here's an example:

"Dear Michael,
"Over the past five years, I have called upon you many times for advice. Your guidance has been enormously valuable to me in my career growth at E.D. Corporation. I am proud to be working in an environment where a high level of product quality and mutual respect between employees and management is the tradition."

Most of us become aware that we want something when we feel its absence. It's difficult to keep from saying: "I'm not happy with my situation, therefore I want . . .". The problem with this is that we are now implying an accusation, that we seem to somehow blame the recipient for not having made us happier. At the emotional level, we are setting up a negative trend in the mind of the recipient. Sometimes we find ourselves thinking, After all, why didn't he or she realize that I deserved this raise, promotion, etc.

If you feel this way, break a vase or something! Then begin your letter with a positive statement. (You'll be starting a positive trend!) For example, say something good about the organization you work for, the person you are writing to, or your work experience in the company. That's why this opening paragraph is called a declaration of loyalty. You want to tell your employers at the outset that you're with them, not against them.

SECOND PARAGRAPH: STATEMENT OF PURPOSE

Make maximum use of the positive climate you've just established, and state your objective briefly but clearly. You want the reader to have an instant favorable reaction to your objective, while reserving judgment on its merits until you've had time to prove your case in the next paragraph.

"My objective in writing to you today is to ask you to consider me for the position of general manager of operations at the new Springfield plant. I feel this would give me an opportunity to substantially increase the range of contributions I can make to our company."

No need to beat around the bush or embellish. Nobody has time to read a long letter, wondering what its purpose is. In clear concise language, state your objective, request, proposal, or whatever it is you want to achieve or want the recipient to do.

THIRD PARAGRAPH: SUPPORTING FACTS

Every request or proposal you make, no matter how reasonable or obvious to you, needs supporting facts in order to convince or persuade another person to take action. Whatever action you wish to be taken, your proposal has to be documented by some form of past achievement and future intent that is related to the proposed objective. While your past achievements testify to your ability, they may not always be related only to your present employer. Your potential contributions must clearly benefit that employer. Here are typical examples of both past accomplishments and future contributions:

"In support of my proposal, I would like to review some of my responsibilities and contributions since I joined the company: created and managed new service department; warehouse manager, vehicle manager, traffic manager, and general manager for the old plant. Each of these positions represented an increase in responsibility. They resulted in specific contributions to the company, such as the recent decrease in employee turnover of 17 percent, compared with two years ago. Elimination of three functions that had duplicated the work of other departments, resulting in an estimated cost saving of $95,000 per year.

"By continuing these activities in my new position, I expect to make tangible contributions in terms of increased productivity and reduced costs. A specific innovation I would like to discuss with you is an employee training and motivation program, using current, sophisticated techniques that have proven successful in other companies similar to ours. If you find my plan acceptable, I can have the program in place by the first of the year."

Note that the person making this proposal has satisfied himself in prior, off-the-record conversations, and that it is in line with his superior's thinking. Whatever your objective, demonstrate two things: *that you merit its achievement, and that it's in the interest of your employer to grant it.* Usually past contributions will demonstrate the first, and intended future contributions will demonstrate the second.

FOURTH PARAGRAPH: THE HUMAN FACTOR

We often forget that none of our actions takes place in a vacuum, especially on the job. Every change in our work affects our environment. And our working environment consists mostly of people. Whenever a decision is made that changes our condition in any way, the person who makes the decision has to consider this effect on others within his or her jurisdiction. For example: If you are asking for, and are given, a promotion to a senior position, someone else might then no longer be in the running for that same position. This might create a problem for your boss. You need to show a willingness to share responsibility for solving that problem. At the very least you can show that you're aware of it. It's one of the clearest ways to show your boss that you're on his or her side and, thereby, reinforce the positive climate you've established at the beginning of your presentation.

"I know you may be concerned with finding someone to fill my current position. I have several candidates in mind that I would like to discuss with you. It is also clear to me that the position of general manager of operations for the new plant is one that will support your responsibility as vice-president of distribution. I want to assure you that I have every intention of working closely with you to determine how I can best accommodate your goals and interests."

Note: This paragraph is not always needed, but it should always be considered.

FIFTH PARAGRAPH: FOLLOW-THROUGH

Without active follow-through, no presentation is worth making. You will certify this document by clearly showing your intention to conclude this process successfully. Remember: There's always a next step. Take the initiative to indicate when and where your next step will take place. Waiting to hear from the recipient is not a reasonable next step, because you give up control of the process. Show that you intend to initiate a follow-up conversation to discuss the merits of your objective and presentation.

Keeping control of the process is the *only* way to guarantee results. This is an important rule to remember throughout your Campaign.

> "I would like to meet with you to discuss this request at your earliest convenience. I'll stop in at your office on Monday morning so we can arrange a mutually convenient time."
>
> Yours sincerely,

In reviewing the first draft of your presentation, you'll find that you harbor some resentment toward your employer for not having taken action sooner, and on his own initiative. You've probably complained to others and are seeing yourself as the injured party. At least slightly! Some of this resentment may well have crept into your first paragraph. Do you recognize phrases like:

> "Now that I've been passed over for a raise three times in a row . . ." or, "I've been employed here for two years, and isn't it about time . . ." or even, "I'm sick and tired of . . ." These are caricatures, of course. Here is a real-life example:

> "Dear Carl,
> After three years of promised advancement here at BQ Industries, I feel the time is appropriate for me to receive a promotion. My performance in the past years

has been outstanding, as you have said yourself many times."

The principle of emotional reciprocity demands that blame is met with blame, accusation provokes counter-accusation. If I'm told I unjustly passed you over for a raise, I'll find a way of proving that you didn't deserve it. You may be right, but you'll also be poor.

Does that mean that you'll be expected to "butter me up" with insincerity even though you feel I've acted unjustly? Not at all! You've deserved a raise, and you'll be able to demonstrate it. By concentrating on the genuinely constructive aspects of our association, you'll generate a positive response on my part. The law of reciprocity in human relations is inexorable, both in the negative and the positive sense.

So, a precondition of a successful presentation is to reality-test the objective you wish to reach *before* writing a presentation. The only way this can be done is through people. Off-the-record discussions with members of your C/I Network will help you at this stage. *After* you've written the first draft of your letter, another check with the same people will tell you if you've made your point and supported your objective convincingly.

The next step is to decide on the time and place to make your presentation and start your In-company Campaign in earnest.

CHAPTER 9

WHEN AND HOW TO ACTIVATE YOUR IN-COMPANY CAMPAIGN

You have now completed your preparation phase and are ready to move into action. You have a clear objective, both in your head and on paper. You can't wait to get started? Good! But there's one more thing you have to consider before you jump: timing.

Control of timing leads to control of results. And at no point in your In-company Campaign should you ever lose control or turn it over to anyone else. This doesn't mean that you can make your superiors do anything that's not in their interest. But you've already taken care of that by choosing a realistic, mutually beneficial objective.

Before you signal the start of your In-company Campaign to your superior, review the following questions to make sure your timing is right.

At the emotional level: Are you in a constructive frame of mind or are you distracted by negative feelings, either about your workplace or problems at home? Is the person for whom your presentation is intended in a positive frame of mind, as far as you know? You'll need all the positive energy you can muster to create the conditions for success.

At the factual level:

Do you see any specific obstacles that should be removed, or conditions that could improve, given a little more time? While we don't recommend procrastination in the hope that some unspecified event will work in your favor, we have seen situations where a postponement of only one or two days removed very specific roadblocks and created significantly more favorable conditions for beginning an In-company Campaign.

Here are two examples of factors that can affect timing decisions:

Anne J. had worked as a claims adjuster during her three years at R.Q. Insurance Co. Her In-company Campaign goal was a promotion to manager of the claims department. She was anxious to start her Campaign, because she knew that the current manager would be leaving in less than two months. Also, the vice-president responsible for filling the position was known to favor recruiting from outside the company, rather than promoting people from within.

Once she made her decision, Anne felt it was crucial to get her Campaign started as quickly as possible. Unfortunately, the vice-president to whom her Campaign was directed had recently had knee surgery and was literally hobbling around the office in pain. At this point he was in no condition to focus on his own work, and probably wouldn't be receptive to Anne's proposal. She wisely decided to wait a few days—until it was clear that the vice-president's pain had subsided.

Alex M.'s In-company Campaign proposal for a salary increase was written and ready for presentation to his boss, the president of a printing company. Alex was an account executive who serviced some of the company's major clients. He had been with the firm a little over one year and had increased sales on his own accounts by 30 percent.

There was only one hitch: The company was heavily in debt due to a move and unprecedented increases in the cost of paper. A loan had been applied for, but no decision would be forthcoming until at least another week. Alex knew he would not be likely to benefit from making his proposal until the loan was transacted.

We want to make it very clear that we never advocate giving up an In-company Campaign at this or any other point. A timing adjustment is a fine-tuning operation, not an either/or decision.

Having decided that the timing is right to the best of your knowledge, your next step is to get your written presentation into the hands of the person to whom it's addressed. You can, of course, put it in that person's mailbox or hand it to his or her secretary. But whenever you are reasonably well acquainted with the person, simply hand it over with the words:

"I've written a proposal . . .
"Here's a letter . . .   } that you
"I've just put some ideas on paper . . .

might find interesting. I'd like to discuss this with you after you've had a chance to study it."

The best timing for this transaction is when there is no temptation or opportunity for the recipient to open the envelope and read your letter on the spot.

Some people feel an obligation to respond instantly, and it's up to you to let them know that you don't expect or want such a response. Instant responses are usually made on the emotional level. They don't allow time for rational thought, consideration, or compromise. They tend to be black or white, all or nothing. Therefore, the end of a work day, or better, the end of a work week is the best time to transmit written In-company Campaign presentations.

To illustrate:

You present your boss with a proposal that includes a large expenditure. It's 1:30 P.M., he's just returned from lunch, and his desk is clear. He opens your letter, reads it on the spot, comes to the dollar signs, and starts to shake his head. Before he even finishes the letter, he looks up and says, "Sorry, but *no way*. We're in no condition to be spending money now! Forget it."

Now let's go back to the starting point and hand in the proposal again:

This time it's 4:00 P.M. on Friday afternoon. You give it to your boss's secretary and say, "I'll call him next week to set up a meeting on this." Now your boss has time to read the letter alone. He gets past the dollar signs and takes in the justification for the expense and the expected benefits.

He's responding rationally now, and you'll get the opportunity to make a "final sale" when you meet in person.

Whatever method and time you choose to transmit your letter, follow it up with a question put to the decision maker a few days later, along the lines:

"Have you had an opportunity to read my letter?" or "Now that you've had a chance to read my letter . . . when would be a good time for us to discuss it?"

Note: You haven't asked for a decision, but for an opportunity to talk! You still have to complete the second half of the communications process—the face-to-face presentation. By closely following the guidelines given here, you'll stay in control of the process.

The first step in preparing for the meeting with your boss or other decision makers is to *assume success*. This is a technique that's known to every salesperson—and for the moment you are making a sale. If you've done everything right up to this point, you are likely to be in the enviable situation of having a "product" that virtually sells itself. You've made sure that your objective makes sense, that it benefits everybody, and that your credentials are in order.

The assumption of success is an important psychological consideration. There is a great temptation at this point to go into a meeting with the boss with words like "I know it's a terrible imposition . . ." or "You wouldn't by any chance consider . . .". We are caricaturing, but the underlying attitude is very common.

Take a few minutes to review, mentally or by rereading a copy of your presentation, what words you used to describe your objective, and the facts you listed in support of it. Be prepared to talk with confidence about what you are trying to achieve.

"I really feel good about what's been happening with our firm lately, and about having been able to play a part in it. . . ."

A second assumption you can safely make is that your meeting may well be the first of several. The more complex your objective, the more discussion is usually needed to achieve it.

> "I'd like to get your reaction to my presentation—I'll be glad to answer any questions you may have." (After a discussion of the proposal.) "I want to give you some time to think about this. Can we meet again next Monday? Do you think you might be able to make a decision by then?" (Guard against pushing for a decision on a complex proposal at the first meeting.)

What responses can you expect? Should you accept any response as a final decision?

Here is a list of possible responses, together with actual examples.

1. The best but not the most frequent response is a simple yes. The only thing for you to do is say thank-you, and enjoy the fruits of your labor. (You may, at this point, begin to suspect that you should have asked for more. Don't worry—there is always a next step! The best possible habit your boss can get into is to say yes to you and to say it often.)

2. The next best, and statistically most frequently given response is "Yes, but . . .". Your boss may see a possible objection which he'll share with you, and which you can help him dispose of, either at the first meeting or at a later one. Or you may receive a counteroffer in the form of a compromise solution, which you'll carefully consider, and either accept or renegotiate further.

> When Anne J. finally made her proposal for a promotion to the manager of the claims department of her insurance company, the V.P. in charge had these objections. First, he was concerned that she'd never actually managed others before. This, he said, was his

reason for generally recruiting managers from outside the company. Second, if he promoted her, he'd be short a claims adjuster, and the work overload in that area was already becoming a problem.

Even with these objections, he was impressed by Anne's performance as documented in her letter, and was willing to consider her proposal. After further discussions at two subsequent meetings, it was agreed that Anne would be given "acting" management responsibility while she trained a new claims adjuster. After two months, her performance as manager would be reviewed and a permanent decision would be made.

A variation on number 2 is "Yes—but not now." Your boss may have ideas on timing that differ from yours.

These ideas may even be more realistic than yours, *but not necessarily*. Your reaction should be to find out (by asking) what your boss had in mind. You will either accept the proposed time delay or attempt to negotiate by giving good reasons for eliminating the delay.

Harry T.'s case is a good example of this kind of negotiating. Recently hired as a salesman for a small but growing pharmaceutical company, he requested a company car. His boss proposed a time delay of at least nine months on the grounds that only the senior salesmen got cars, and Harry's territory wasn't very large yet. Harry proposed that the company give him a car on a trial basis for three months. During this period, Harry would expand his territory and increase sales to justify the decision, or the car would be returned. Harry had enough sales experience to be confident about making this kind of deal. His boss went for it.

In some cases your superior will want to see something happen (e.g. a more profitable month for the company) or you will be expected to do something (e.g. complete a project) before you are given the final yes. In both cases you will want to consider agreeing to the time delay, provided that the agreement on your objective is spelled out and the timing is defined specifically.

Philip S., for instance, had proposed that he hire an assistant for himself. As financial manager for a commercial real estate firm, he found that he could no longer handle the regular accounting function, together with the financial planning and negotiating, within a reasonably long work day.

The president of the company agreed that Philip's proposal was valid, but asked him to wait "a couple of months." Philip asked if there were a specific reason for waiting. He learned that the president didn't want to hire additional staff until the end of the company's fiscal year. Philip agreed that waiting made sense under the circumstances but asked for a specific date to hire his assistant. The president had no problem with this.

3. Another possible response to your presentation is noncommittal. "I'll have to give this more thought" or "I'm not sure what you're proposing is feasible." This is a perfectly reasonable response, especially if your objective is ambitious. The response should be taken literally. More thought may be needed, and you can help guide the thinking by strengthening your argument during subsequent meetings (see chapter 10 on follow-through).

Florence G. was the assistant to the director of advertising at a small but rapidly expanding publishing company. She was hired largely on the basis of her background in art, but discovered that most of the work in this area was doled out to agencies or free-lancers. Her In-company Campaign objective was to create and become the director of an in-house art department.

She made her presentation to both the director of advertising and the president of the company. They were impressed with her background and had little concern about her capabilities. They were nevertheless uncertain about how this could be accomplished without costing the company a great deal of additional money in salaries. They voiced their doubts. Florence suggested a second meeting. During the next meeting, Florence presented complete information on the comparison between the company's fees paid to freelance artists and agencies as opposed to a full-time staff. She also showed how permanent staffing and faster turn-around in the art and graphics area would increase the company's overall capacity to handle more work, handle it more efficiently, and make greater profits.

Florence's perseverance in communicating the feasibility of her In-company Campaign goal ultimately influenced her superiors to see things her way.

4. A fourth type of response may be a negative answer, such as "I don't think we're in a position to grant your request." It should never be accepted as a turn-off. Remember, you have carefully researched your objective. The fact that it makes sense to you, but not to your boss, means that you and your boss see things differently. The logical next step is to find out why. You can always discover (again, by asking) what the obstacle is. This knowledge gives you the power to find a way, or help your boss find a way, around it. Sometimes your boss will immediately describe the obstacle preventing him from making a positive decision. This in itself is usually a sign that he will accept help in finding a way out of the difficulty. An assumption of success on your part will often make the difference.

Convince your boss that it's worthwhile to go to some trouble to make possible the achievement of your proposed objective.

Marian J., for example, had asked for a substantial mid-year salary increase. As executive secretary to the vice-president of operations, she had carefully documented her contributions and believed her request quite reasonable. When her boss said, "I'm sorry, but I can't give you this kind of a raise," Marian assumed that her boss undervalued her work. Fortunately, she did not act on this assumption, but decided to find out (by asking) what influenced her boss's decision.

Her boss was perfectly open about it: "If you get this kind of a raise, you'll be making more than any other executive secretary in the company. That would create a lot of problems."

Marian thought about this objection and worked out a number of possible solutions that she then presented to her boss:

She could get her raise half in money and half in fringe benefits. This approach would alleviate the problem of outstripping the salaries of the other executive secretaries, while providing her with compensation for her work through additional benefits.

The second suggestion was to award Marian the salary increase, and justify it by basing it strictly on the additional level of productivity she had carefully documented. This might not entirely solve the problem, but it did have the advantage that the company could use her salary increase as an incentive to others. They could be in line for the same income if they produced at the same level.

Finally, Marian presented the idea of changing her job definition and title to reflect her additional contribution. Because she had taken on the responsibility of coordinating and analyzing all of the administrative quality-control reports, she suggested the title of "Quality-Control Administrator."

Marian's boss was receptive to her proposal and impressed with her effort. He told her he'd need a few days to see which approach would be most acceptable.

Ultimately, he agreed to giving her the increase half in money and half in upgrading her fringe benefits. She was also promised favorable consideration for the title of "Quality-Control Administrator."

It is possible, of course, that your boss sees you in a completely different light from that in which you see yourself. He or she may never have communicated this to you or anyone else. That's why you didn't know about it, and couldn't possibly prepare for it. Here is a typical example of how this can happen:

You joined your firm as a part-time employee and, during the preemployment interview, mentioned that you wouldn't be available for full-time work because of other interests in your life. You may have changed your mind in the meantime but neglected to communicate this to your boss. If you plan your In-company Campaign and make your proposal based on a full-time work concept, you would have little credibility. Your boss hadn't been aware of how, when, or why you changed your mind about full-time work.

You may feel that your proposal and the fact that you gradually increased your working hours were sufficient evidence for your changed self-concept.

In fact this rarely happens. A change in attitude toward your work or your employer takes a long time to communicate itself if left to chance. Sometimes years. Both in the positive and negative direction.

You have to speed up the process if you want to reap the benefits. Sometimes changing your employer's image of you can be done in purposeful daily communications over a period of time, and sometimes a mini-In-company Campaign is the better and quicker way.

This is an important point and we'll illustrate it with two examples:

David K. was an avid union supporter in the electronics assembly plant where he worked. After two years of doing competent assembly work, David showed interest in moving into a supervisory position. Unfortunately, his superiors thought this was pretty funny, since David had spent the better part of his work days for two years promoting unions.

As it became obvious that he had a real image problem with his bosses, David determined to build his credibility for a management position by taking on extra duties on his own initiative. He offered to train other assembly workers and asked to be allowed to sit in at management meetings. After six months of working on his relationships, making responsible and constructive suggestions, and showing consistent concern for the company, David was offered a position as assistant plant manager.

This is an example of a campaign without a written presentation. But not without a plan and follow-up! An image change can sometimes take a long time. The next example shows how this process can be speeded up with a well-directed In-company Campaign.

As a successful account executive in a large advertising agency, Janis J. was shocked to learn she was passed over for a promotion she was sure she deserved. The circumstances made her think about her image, and she realized she'd been talking about her new baby and her family activities almost exclusively for the past few months.

Janis prepared a written presentation for a promotion, making it clear that she was recommitting herself to the goals of the organization. She supported the proposal with substantial examples of her capabilities and numerous contributions to the firm.

During a subsequent meeting with her superiors, Janis convinced them of her ability to perform and her seriousness about her job. Consistent follow-through soon earned her the well-deserved promotion.

5. Occasionally the response is a definite and categorical no. In our experience, when that happens, it's because an important fact was not known to the person making the presentation, such as an imminent corporate merger which puts all internal changes on hold. Again, the first step is to find out the reason for the response, then to make a decision on further action. In the event of a clear no, your choices are to:

- Reimplement the In-company Campaign at a later time when conditions have changed
- Switch to a different but equally desirable objective
- Reach the original objective in two or more small steps, one at a time, or
- Discontinue all efforts.

This last choice is synonymous with a decision to leave the organization. A job in which you have no freedom or movement is, by definition, the wrong job. However, better than half of the people who have encountered this problem and who have used the methods described in this book have found that their correct application enabled them to start moving again within their current organizations.

With the exception of an unqualified yes, all the types of responses described above can usually be turned into successful outcomes by consistent and skillful follow-through. This skill is described in the next chapter. It's not difficult to learn, and is based, as is everything else in this book, on commonsense methods of human relations, with a dash of persistence thrown in.

CHAPTER 10

ACTIVE FOLLOW-THROUGH: THE KEY TO SUCCESS

Let's take another look at the overall purpose of conducting an In-company Campaign. We have heard
people talk about their work in terms of "not actually
hating it" all the way to "loving it, being inspired by it,
and ultimately inspiring others with it." The intermediate terms on this scale include "finding the work not
bad, okay, pleasant, satisfying, fulfilling."

Our point in listing these terms is to show that,
wherever you are on this scale, there is always a higher
level you can achieve, a next step you can take. No In-
company Campaign will ever take you all the way in
one step.

By definition any campaign has a beginning and an
end. But there is no limit to the number of campaigns
you can undertake. In fact each campaign will be easier than the previous one conducted successfully in the
same organization. Provided, of course, that it results
in tangible benefits to both you and the organization.
This is due, in part, to the human relations principle

mentioned in an earlier chapter: Your employer needs to validate his or her decisions. *Every time your boss makes a decision in your favor, he or she'll go on to help you prove that the decision was justified and deserved.*

You not only get ahead because you are perceived to be good at what you do, you are also perceived to be good at what you do because you get ahead—you look like a person on the move!

In chapter 9 we talked about presenting your In-company Campaign. Now we'll show how to bring it to a successful conclusion. Any In-company Campaign consists (in equal portions) of a realistic and achievable objective, a presentation that proves the soundness of the objective, and the follow-through action necessary to achieve the objective.

Follow-through is the most neglected ingredient of a successful campaign. Here are some statements that should sound familiar to you:

> "My boss agreed that if my sales record remained as high as it has been for six months, I'd get promoted to sales manager. That was over six months ago, and I haven't got my promotion yet."

> "I wrote my boss a memo to remind him it was time for my yearly raise. I even listed my accomplishments. He said he was very impressed with my work, but I haven't seen an extra nickel in my paycheck."

> "I keep telling my boss I need an assistant. I've presented my case in great detail, and he agrees with me completely. The problem is, he never does anything about it."

The missing element in these examples is the follow-through action. Tacit acceptance of objections is the opposite of follow-through.

How many steps should you expect to have to go

through to achieve the result? As many steps as it takes. How much time should you allow? As much time as it takes. An In-company Campaign is either successful or it isn't! But you won't know which until it's completed. And the only unsuccessful campaign is the one that ends in a complete and categorical NO. Even then you can "live to fight another day!"

Compromises are frequently considered acceptable results. Here are some examples of acceptable compromises.

Monroe G. was office manager in a large law firm. His In-company Campaign goal had been a substantial salary increase. His compromise was to receive half now and half in six months. During this time, he was expected to improve his relationship with one of the firm's partners and revamp the company's filing system.

Carol C. worked for a consumer research organization where she had managed a variety of projects for three years. Her In-Company Campaign goal was to become manager of her research division. Her compromise was to accept the position of associate manager. She would be responsible for all research projects in her division, while another associate manager would handle all administrative and personnel procedures.

Virginia K. had proposed a raise for herself. She was administrative assistant to a senior vice-president at a national manufacturing firm. Her compromise was to accept half the raise in money and half in fringe benefits. Her boss felt this approach would alleviate potential problems with Virginia's counterparts in other departments, all of whom earned less than she did.

The following campaign was seen as unsuccessful by the person involved:

Adam K. had worked at a financial investment firm for four years and was now handling complete portfolios.

Nevertheless he still had not been made a portfolio manager. His boss maintained that this was a reflection of the company policy requiring all managers to have a college business degree. Adam's frustration over his inability to get the title he felt he deserved caused his relationship with his boss to go sour.

Adam's In-company Campaign goal was to get the title "Portfolio Manager." In order to do so, he had to start mending his fences with his boss. Over the next four months, Adam succeeded at opening up the lines of communication, getting more high-level assignments, and even created a feeling of camaraderie with his boss. On the subject of title change, however, Adam found his boss unmovable. Adam could get more money and good assignments, but on the title change he got a definite no.

Adam felt that this was a signal of a dead end in his advancement possibilities with this company, and decided to leave. Although he did not meet his In-company Campaign goal, he had improved his relationship with his boss to such a great extent that he left on a very positive note. His boss offered to give him a good reference and invited him to come back to his old job at any time. It was clear to Adam, and to everyone else, that he was leaving the company for a positive reason (career growth) rather than a negative one. As you can see from this example, even an unsuccessful Campaign can be a forward step in career advancement.

Let's look at the follow-through process in more detail. The timing of any follow-through meetings is usually determined at the previous meeting. At the end of your face-to-face presentation, ask a question:

- "When do you think you'll make your decision?"
- "Can we get together again early next week (tomorrow, the first of next month, etc.) to talk about my proposal?"

- "I'd like to think about the problem you mentioned (your counterproposal, etc.). Can we meet again tomorrow?"
- "I realize you are very busy right now and need time to consider my request. Can I call you next week to set up another meeting?"

None of these requests can be reasonably refused. And you've made sure that the process continues.

Unless your proposal is accepted completely at the time it is first presented, one or more follow-through meetings will have to take place. This is a normal part of the process.

A typical follow-through meeting will have a structure somewhat like this:

1. Make a statement (or restatement) of your proposed objective. Unless your boss calls the meeting, it's up to you to initiate the conversation and state the meeting's purpose.
2. Listen carefully to the other person's response.
3. After taking a minute to consider the response, continue the conversation in one of two ways:
   a) If your superior's response is positive, you will discuss the timing of its implementation and, of course, express your satisfaction.

   For example, "I really appreciate your thoughtfulness and the positive response you've given me. Can we set a date for my promotion? I'd like to take on the new responsibilities as soon as possible."

   b) If the response is neutral or negative, you need to take the time to consider your reaction—to prevent an unconsidered negative emotional response. Then propose the next step.

   For instance: "I think I understand your position. I'd like to think about this further, and get back to you with some new ideas."

4. Remembering that there is always a next step, and

that it isn't possible, in most cases, to plan your response to every possible objection that may come up, ask for another meeting to: a) give some thought to the other person's objection; and b) propose a way to overcome or get around the objection. Some examples are:

"What you say about the company's salary structure makes sense. I'd like to review some ideas I have and meet with you again."

Or: "I realize you may be concerned that this promotion would leave a gap in the department where I'm working. I'd like to meet with you again to discuss how we could handle this without creating problems."

Don't try short-order cooking at this point. Even if you have an argument ready, you'll sound more convincing if you take time to prepare for another meeting. You may, however, want to ask one or two more questions to get a clear idea of your boss's position.

5. Propose or ask for a specific date and time for the next meeting, no matter how long the time interval is or how uncertain everybody's schedule is.

"Can we meet next Friday, the tenth, to continue this discussion? Is 10:30 good for you?"

Many In-company Campaigns have disappeared in the sands of time because this tiny but vital step wasn't taken. If you get unusual resistance at this point, you can at least get an agreement on the week in which the next meeting will happen, and then ask for a specific time later, at the beginning of that week.

One person we know who had a particularly good rapport with his boss used a unique method to nail down the date suggested by his boss: He flipped through his boss's desk calendar and wrote his own initials next to that date. Of course, this is a pretty bold approach and might backfire if you used it with a person you don't know very well.

Suggesting a meeting a few weeks away is often less

threatening to your boss than pressing for an immediate date. Once the commitment is made to see you, it's unlikely that you'll be put off.

6. Before ending a follow-up meeting, make sure it's clear to both you and the other person what each of you is going to do between this and the next meeting.

For instance, it may have been decided that your promotion will be postponed until you get your degree. Restate this at the end of your meeting: "Can we set a date to meet in March? I'll have my degree finished then, and we can talk about my promotion in more concrete terms."

Or, if a raise has been put off because your boss says she needs more information about her budget allowance, you could suggest, "Why don't we meet next Friday, to give you more time to review the information?"

7. Do your part of the "homework" prior to the next meeting or conversation with your boss.

According to the categories of response listed in chapter 9, the following are appropriate types of follow-through action:

Boss's Response to Your Objective	*Your Next Step*
"Yes."	Write a thank-you note or letter. Include your understanding of a specific date (and manner, if applicable) of implementation.
"Yes, but . . ."	Research the best way to meet and/or dispose of the objection. Your C/I

Boss's Response to Your Objective	*Your Next Step*
	Network can help you in this. You may not agree with your boss's objection, or you may see it as an excuse (see chapter 11). But it will nevertheless be an expression of reality from the other person's point of view, and will have to be dealt with.
"There is something I want you to do first."	Make sure you understand what you are asked to do, allow time to do it well, no matter how long it takes, and be sure to document (or let people know) that you are doing it.
"The time isn't right just now."	Find out what factors affect the timing and propose a realistic but reasonably short time delay for implementing your objective. This can either be tied to an event (when the company is profitable) or to a date (first of next month/year, etc.).
"Your proposal is not acceptable in this form" or "I don't understand what you are proposing."	Rewrite your proposal based on a conversation about the reasons for the objection or uncertainty.

Boss's Response to Your Objective	*Your Next Step*
"I'll have to give this some thought."	Reinforce your proposed objective with more facts. Always take positive initiative in follow-through action, never a wait-and-see attitude.
"I don't think what you are proposing/asking is feasible."	Find out reasons. Gather information for a different proposal or for achieving your original objective in two or more smaller steps. Or invite your boss to make a counterproposal that you can then consider.
"NO." (Because of something you didn't know/weren't aware of.)	Find out more about the reason for the turn-down. Consider your next step as unemotionally as you can. Always assume that there *will be* a next step.

Every meeting during an In-company Campaign should be followed by a thank-you note, letter, or statement. Whenever possible or reasonable, send a written acknowledgment, even if it's an informal, handwritten note. In many cases a formal, typed letter is in order. Do the following in your thank-you letter or note:

1. Thank the person for his or her consideration of your proposal, and for the time and effort involved.
2. Restate the follow-through action you intend to take, or the one you expect him or her to take.

3. Confirm the date and time of the next meeting (if any).

Put as much enthusiasm and optimism into the letter as you can muster, compatible with your personal style. Follow-through notes are the most energy-efficient way to fuel your campaign and to assure its beneficial outcome. They are an excellent way to prevent emotional downturns and inject an expectation of success into the In-company Campaign.

Dear Martin,
Thank you for your time and consideration of my proposal for a promotion to project manager. I really appreciate the effort you've made to review my situation and listen to my presentation.
While you are discussing my proposal with the other members of the management team, I will develop a plan to have my present responsibilities taken over, without any time loss to the project completion.
I look forward to meeting with you again on the thirteenth of this month.

Dear Laura,
Thank you for your openness and the time you have spent to discuss my proposal for a salary increase. Your frankness has helped me to understand the concerns of the firm's management and board members.
I will be restructuring my proposal according to the priorities we discussed, as well as including more of my accomplishments that relate to the board's concerns.
I look forward to presenting my revised proposal for the board's approval at the end of the month.

Many people like to see each In-company Campaign as a learning experience and keep a log of the entire sequence of events, including copies of the written presentation and the follow-through notes. Here is an example:

In-company Campaign Objective: Promotion to assistant vice-president—June, 19__

June 6   Letter to request meeting placed in boss's mailbox.
June 11   Presentation to boss—verbal and written.
June 17   Discussion with boss about timing of promotion.
June 18   Memo to boss about June 17 meeting and the decisions made. Restate boss's commitment to announce promotion on June 30.
June 21   Discussion with boss regarding need to recruit replacement for my position.
June 30   Promotion accomplished—invited to dinner with boss.

One word of caution: Follow-through is seen by some as a variation on the broken-record syndrome. The following caricature illustrates what we mean:

Employee: I want a raise!
Boss: Why?
Employee: Because I've been here a year. I'm entitled to a raise.
Boss: But you haven't accomplished anything.
Employee: I've shown up for work every day. I want a raise.
Boss: Business is bad right now.
Employee: That's not my problem; I want a raise.
Boss: I'll think about it.
Employee: I'm behind in my car payments; I need a raise now.
Boss: (Expletive deleted.)

We recognize that this example doesn't apply to any of our readers! It's the result of a misunderstood form of assertiveness training. A person using a more intelligent form of assertiveness would: a) base the request for a raise on documented contributions rather than attendance; b) time it to coincide with business upswing, or be flexible on timing—within limits (accepting a delay, but asking for the effective date to be made retroactive); and c) cite value to the employer rather than private need or personal poverty as compelling reasons.

When does your In-company Campaign end? When you have achieved the best possible result. When do you stop planning and carrying out In-company Campaigns? When you have achieved your ideal work situation. However, because your work situation will change on the day *after* you have achieved perfection, the more accurate answer is: Never! In view of this, it's absolutely necessary to make In-company Campaigns a positive experience. Once you have developed your skill in this area, and see it in terms of benefiting both you and your employer equally, only then will you view the In-company Campaign as a work/life habit and a means of interacting with your job environment, leading to job fulfillment.

CHAPTER 11

SO YOUR CASE IS DIFFERENT: TROUBLESHOOTING YOUR IN-COMPANY CAMPAIGN

Just as there is always a *next step* in an In-company Campaign, there is a solution to every problem, whether it arises during the planning, the implementation, or the follow-up stage. But, you may say, my case is different from all the examples given in this book.

Yes, your situation is different from all others. Your problems are different, your boss is different, your organization is different, the people you work with are different. In fact, they are unique. What's more important, *you* are unique. A standard approach to a set of standard problems would only get a standard response. You are building your case and your presentation on this very uniqueness, in the positive sense, of your personality, your situation, and your contributions. That's why In-company Campaigns work.

Let's say you have asked for a salary increase or a promotion, and you've been summarily turned down. You've followed all the rules, your work is up-to-date, your work relationships are good, your presentation shows clearly that you've earned your increase or promotion—in fact you can't see any reason for such an irrational response. At the emotional level, your reaction will be approximately equal parts of disappointment and resentment. At the rational level, the next step would be to ask three questions in this order: 1) What happened? 2) Why did it happen? 3) What will I do about it?

There's no way to deny or eliminate the emotional reaction. But you can learn to accept it as natural, shorten its duration, and get on with the problem-solving process.

Each In-company Campaign problem has its own peculiar and unique aspects. This leads to a common reaction: "Nobody I know has ever had this problem. I don't understand it. I don't know what to do about it."

The reason for this natural reaction is that In-company Campaign problems are mostly "people problems." They are less capable of being seen clearly and categorized than are mechanical problems.

However, In-company Campaign problems do fall into several main categories. Recognizing these categories will make it easier for you to design your own solution for each problem as it arises.

First, there are *artificial* problems. Artificial problems are rooted in mind-set, attitude, or precedent only. They usually have nothing to do with your ability to perform the job you want to be promoted to, or your having earned the reward you ask for. An example is:

"I know I won't get the raise. My boss has never recognized my value to the company."

This statement does not imply that you don't deserve a raise or that your boss is unable to give you one. It has to do with your attitude toward your boss, or his perceived attitude toward you. There's no reason why you shouldn't go ahead with an In-company Campaign to show that you merit a raise.

This statement also shows an artificial obstacle can be purely emotional. It may only exist in your mind, or it may exist in your employer's mind. It may even be shared by you and your employer:

"My boss and I both know that the other secretaries would resent it if I get promoted to office supervisor, and they won't respect me in the position."

Again, this problem is not related to your ability to do the job. All the statement says is that you have to be sensitive to the effect your In-company Campaign has on others in your job environment.

Anticipated obstacles are a specific type of artificial In-company Campaign problem. Here is an example:

"I know what my boss is going to say. He'll tell me it's against corporate policy to give anyone a salary increase after six months on the job."

This is also an artificial problem because it refers to precedent rather than merit. There's nothing as unprofitable as making up someone else's mind for him or her in advance, yet this is *the single most prevalent reason* why "Enterprises of great pith and moment turn awry, and lose the name of action."

Boss's response to a course of action you have proposed: "But we've never promoted anyone without an MBA to marketing manager."

While this may be a statement of fact, it refers to past history and is not necessarily a real obstacle to promoting a person who is capable of doing the job. It's a problem of perception and belongs in the category of artificial problems. Here is how James M., a sales representative for a tire manufacturing company, dealt with this problem during his In-company Campaign:

> In his position for five years, James had contributed much to the firm, such as training other sales representatives, introducing new products, expanding his sales territory, and increasing sales at a significant rate each quarter. Nevertheless, his boss's initial reaction to James's presentation to become a marketing manager was, "You don't have a degree. Our marketing managers have always had an MBA, and I don't know how I can convince the board of directors to make an exception."
>
> James responded to this by preparing a carefully documented, written presentation listing his contributions. With an abundant supply of these achievements, which were directly applicable to the job of marketing manager, James had given his boss exactly what was needed to convince the others of his value. Armed with real evidence of James's ability to do the job, his boss now felt comfortable giving James the promotion and presenting the decision to the board.

Once this type of objection has been stated in so many words, it can be overcome, because it requires only a change in mind-set or attitude (or a change in a policy based on precedent which, in this case, is the same thing!). This kind of artificial problem should never be a reason *not* to start an In-company Campaign.

Factual problems are another category of In-company Campaign obstacles. Here are some examples:

"I want to be promoted to marketing manager, but I know that the other person considered for the job has five years' seniority."

You know before you start writing your presentation that this can certainly be a real obstacle (rules of seniority are not usually considered an artificial mind-set or arbitrary policy) and has to be planned for in the Campaign preparation. If you feel, for instance, that your qualifications for the job are strong enough to override rules of seniority, document that in your presentation.

Note that the "factual" in this case means only that there are tangible circumstances or conditions (rather than more or less emotional assumptions made by you or others) that you have to deal with, not that these are reasons for abandoning your In-company Campaign.

Halfway through your In-company Campaign, the person you've been talking with leaves the company. This is certainly a factual problem. What do you do next? Do you start all over again with someone else?

There are a number of circumstances that, like this one, will force you to review your strategy and sometimes change course. This is a normal part of In-company Campaigning. Think of strategy reviews and course changes as *logical next steps,* not as "being in trouble." Focus your emotions positively by thinking in terms of challenges instead of problems.

Once again, the difference between artificial and factual problems is that artificial problems are rooted in assumption, tradition, precedent, or mind-set. Don't accept them as facts, but be aware that you must plan for dealing with the assumptions or mind-set, both in yourself and others.

Factual problems, on the other hand, are real obstacles that must be accepted. In those cases you'll have to find a way around them, either when you plan your presentation or when they come up during your campaign. To further illustrate the difference between artificial and factual In-company Campaign problems: An unschooled hospital orderly who wishes to be promoted to brain surgeon faces a factual problem, while a woman brain surgeon who is denied a promotion to chief of surgery on the grounds that a woman has never held the position is clearly confronted with an artificial problem. This isn't to say that artificial problems are always easy to overcome, especially if they're based on long-established prejudices.

Being a member of one or more minority groups may make you subject to one particular type of artificial problem: negative discrimination. Eli Djeddah, in his excellent book *Moving Up*, has written:

"Grounds for discrimination are innumerable and the situation is complicated by the fact that every group that is discriminated against, in its turn, discriminates against others. If you are black or white, Chinese, Indian, Puerto Rican, Spanish, Irish, or Italian; Communist, Birchite, Democrat, or Republican; a hawk or a dove; homosexual, lesbian, hermaphrodite, or sexless; fat or thin, short or tall, bald or hairy; one-legged or one-armed; very old or very young; blind, deaf, or mute; blue-, brown-, or hazel-eyed; squinting, stuttering, or muttering; Catholic, Jewish, Protestant, Muhammadan, Buddhist, or atheist; and are in fact alive, you are likely to be discriminated against by some group, somewhere, at some time."

While discrimination is a fact of life, it needn't be a deterrent to action. Your attitude is the key. For every negative aspect of discrimination, there is a positive one. You would not take your boss to court for being prejudiced in your favor—for believing that you can walk on water, move mountains, or successfully complete any task assigned to you. So, for every negative prejudice, there is a corresponding positive one. Here are some examples of positive word associations in place of negative ones:

Negative	Positive
Too young	Energetic, flexible, full of potential
Too old	Experienced, wise
Fat	Impressive, dignified
Thin	Lean, agile, active
Handicapped	Hard worker, conscientious

Prejudices, positive or negative, etc. tend to be assumptions made at the emotional level, and may not have any foundation in reality. But because emotions are very much part of reality, we have to be aware of these prejudices and, wherever possible, channel them into a positive direction. Fortunately, we have many tools available to use for this purpose. Attitude and behavior are the most effective tools, but auxiliary means such as dress, cosmetics, and physical condition can be used to create a favorable image as well.

If you're overweight, for example, you wouldn't expect to make a dignified or impressive presentation by wearing tight, clinging, or poorly tailored clothing. (We know one successful person who has been getting away with it for years, but he is a genius. If you're a genius you can break many rules!)

On the other hand, a stout person with erect posture, wearing a neatly pressed, dark suit, can create an impression of dignity and stature.

What you wear and how you appear physically reveals your attitude almost as much as what you say. If you feel others may see you as being too young for the position to which you aspire, don't come to work chewing gum and wearing the latest fad acessories.

The only way you'll be taken seriously is if you look and act as purposeful as you say you are. To a large extent, you can control the way others perceive you.

Discrimination for reasons over which you have no control is more difficult to deal with. If you are a member of a group to whom access to certain professions or professional levels has traditionally been denied (this group is so large that we refuse to call it a "minority" group), your first step is to find out whether or not there is evidence of prejudice or discrimination in your case. Don't allow yourself to make the assumption automatically. Remember, at the emotional level we tend to see everything as all or nothing. Unlike being pregnant, it is possible to be a little bit prejudiced, a condition that can be overcome with a few facts.

If you allow yourself to remain at the emotional level of reaction to real or imagined discrimination, your negative attitude will force you into a negative trend. The person responsible for discriminatory action will feel justified and you will have allowed prejudice to defeat you.

> Glenn S. had asked for a raise, but his boss turned him down, citing poor business conditions as a reason. Soon after, Glenn learned that two of his coworkers had been given the raises they had requested. His reaction was: "My boss is obviously prejudiced against me. Why should I work as hard as I do?"
>
> So Glenn stopped working so hard, and soon his boss felt quite justified in not having given him the raise.

The moral of this story is twofold: First, even if Glenn's boss *weren't* prejudiced, now he certainly isn't going to give a raise to someone who doesn't work very hard; and second, if the boss *were* prejudiced, Glenn's slowdown helped to justify the prejudice.

How do you know whether or not real discrimination is at work? You have some tools available to you. One is your C/I Network. Other people can make a much more objective judgment of this factor than you.

But use common sense while soliciting the views of others for your own information. Don't use their confidential statements to you as a club with which to beat your superiors into submission.

> Allison P., for instance, asked for a promotion to department manager at the large retail store where she worked. Her boss rejected the proposal, stating that the company's policy was that department managers must be at least thirty years old. Allison discussed this with a few people in her C/I Network, including one of her boss's closest associates, Frank J. She learned from Frank that there was, in fact, no such company tradition.
>
> Allison took this information right back to her boss, righteously declaring, "Frank told me that there isn't any age policy. Why are you discriminating against me? I think you are really being very unfair."
>
> Needless to say, Allison's approach didn't make any points with her boss and Frank wasn't too anxious to talk with her after that.

A second tool is the conversion of a negative prejudice into a positive one.

Because racial, religious, or sex prejudice, and even academic and professional prejudice, are group or class prejudices, they are easily overcome by facts pertaining to individuals. We have all heard references to a person as being much more intelligent . . . well dressed . . . affluent . . . honest . . . open minded . . . or articulate . . . than you'd expect from someone of his or her class, religion, race, or national origin. An example of this kind of conversion is seen in Kathy M's case:

> As inventory-control supervisor for a national merchandising operation, Kathy aspired to become a trav-

eling salesperson for the company. She was familiar with many of the customers the company supplied, knew the inventory, and was very skilled at customer relations. But the company's vice-president of sales had never "put a woman on the road before."

Kathy spent over a year developing her relationships with the bigger customers and making merchandising suggestions that clearly resulted in increased sales. She reported her accomplishments regularly to the vice-president of sales and ultimately was rewarded with his declaration: "It's clear you're handling your job just like a man would."

Back-handed as the compliment seemed, Kathy had set herself outside the structure of the prejudice that was her only barrier to becoming a member of the sales force. Now perceived as an "exceptional woman," her proposal was taken seriously.

Another expression, illustrating the ability to accept individuals while discriminating against the groups from which they come, is: "Some of my best friends are . . .". The main objective is to see yourself, and to get your employer to see you, as a unique individual. The In-company Campaign methodology outlined in this book is the best tool available for this purpose. In fact, it's almost impossible to determine if real prejudice is at work without having applied these methods.

The rule of thumb here is: *Don't assume prejudice!* Discrimination is just one of the problems that you'll deal with in the normal follow-through process; a bridge to be crossed when you come to it.

Is it proper to turn prejudice in your favor? To be the token woman, token black, token Hispanic in a profession or organization? Yes, provided you give value for money earned. Many so-called token employees have pioneered entry into certain professions and job categories through outstanding performance in the job (and judicious In-company Campaigns!).

What if blind, unreasonable, and unrelenting job discrimination is evident? Many forms of discrimination are against the law, and legal redress is available. However, consider your planned legal action carefully. It will put you in an adversary relationship with your employer. Whether you win or lose, legal action means that you will have to carefully rebuild your work relationships with others, provided you wish to stay with your employer. For that reason, legal redress is not usually thought of as a means to improve your current job situation, unless you plan—and expect to manage—the consequences. To illustrate:

Margaret S. was a reporter for a small-town newspaper. She believed she had a good case for sex discrimination on the basis of comparisons between her salary and the salaries of male coworkers. Although she wanted to be paid fairly, she didn't want to leave her job or create more problems for herself.

Margaret was advised by her lawyer that she had grounds for legal action. She filed suit and, realizing that this action could cause a great deal of personal hostility between her and her employer, made every effort to avoid starting a negative trend. She displayed a fully cooperative attitude at work, and made a point of being polite and conversational with her boss. In fact, she even stated to her boss that the legal suit was a separate matter and that she didn't expect it to interfere with her work in any way.

When she won the case, she thanked her employer for the financial recompense he gave her, even though he was ordered by the court to do so.

"But my profession is different." We often hear the statement that, in certain professions, tradition precludes application of the approach described here.

Professors say: "In my profession you just wait for tenure, and it takes x years to get it." Lawyers say:

"The legal profession is governed by certain rules and everybody has to abide by them." (Such as not advertising—a tradition now in the process of being broken.)

In fact, the most traditional aspect of any profession is the involvement of *people,* with their common attitudes, prejudices, thoughts, and feelings.

One of the special rules for In-company Campaigners in tradition-ridden professions is the emphasis on expanding their C/I Network beyond their employing organization—to professional societies, and throughout their entire profession. Justin K.'s example illustrates this technique:

> He had been associated with his law firm for many years, sitting tight and waiting to be invited to become a partner. When he realized he wasn't going to get it just by waiting, he began to discuss the situation with a couple of senior colleagues at local bar association meetings. From these discussions, he learned that bringing more business into the firm and cultivating some political connections in his community would help to make him a candidate for promotion to a partnership.
>
> In fact, Justin had already become a member of his town council, but hadn't made it known in his firm. By sharing this information, and asking for political advice, he was able to present himself in a new light.

"My boss is different" is often said by people who have tried and failed to gain advancement within their organization. If this is your situation, try to remember the circumstances. Did you follow *all* the steps outlined in chapter 7?

If you feel that your superior's personality and temperament make you doubtful about the wisdom of starting an In-company Campaign, don't be discouraged. Even though the techniques in this book are designed around common denominators shared by people, we also show how their individual idiosyncrasies can be dealt with. For instance, a boss who dislikes reading long reports needs to receive a short, punchy presentation. Fact-oriented people need to get facts. Idealistic people want to hear about future benefits of your proposed objectives, while a down-to-earth boss needs to be told about short-term, nuts-and-bolts results.

A memo to the idealistic boss might start out as follows:

"I would like to meet with you next Friday, at a mutually convenient time, to review our goals for the department and to be sure I'm in tune with your ideas for company growth."

While a down-to-earth, nuts-and-bolts person might read:

"Can we set a time for a meeting on Friday to talk about:
1. Department Goals
2. Employee Relations
3. Corporate Growth.
"I've prepared a list of specific proposals I'd like to discuss with you."

Let's say your boss is "impossible." That usually means his or her thought processes are beyond your ability to understand, or at least to feel in tune with. Finding the wavelength of a person alien to your set of values is a real challenge, although not impossible. Disregard, for the purpose of this exercise, how you feel about your boss. Use your C/I Network, and all the objectivity you can muster, to discover his or her operating mode. You will find that you can deal effectively with people with whom you have nothing in common. You may be an intellectually oriented person, for example, and feel that your boss is crude and insensitive.

> Dorothy N., a bookkeeper for a dry-cleaning store owner, felt this way. She had little to talk about with her boss until she learned to her considerable surprise that he had recently developed an interest in opera. On the basis of this information she started discussing her favorite opera with her boss. Eventually, she modified her personal opinion of him.

Your task will never be to "change a person," but to accept who the person is and to change your *relationship* with him or her. Invariably, with almost every person, you'll find at least one area in which you are in agreement or in tune (see chapter 4).

One of the most difficult but also one of the most important human relations skills you can develop is to see things from the other person's point of view. How would you do his job? Better? Of course! But how? Think about it. Take into account all the factors your boss has to deal with in the course of a normal day. Understudy him or her. You'll find that you'll develop understanding and empathy for your boss's position. This, in turn, will give you the information you need to make a presentation that gets your boss's attention.

> Jose V. used this method to develop his proposal for management responsibility at the bank he worked in. Careful observation of his boss, the bank's manager, resulted in the discovery that the boss enjoyed dealing with customers and using his skills in financial planning, loan decisions, and solving credit problems, but hated getting involved in hiring, firing, and training of personnel. Jose, who had been an administrative assist-

ant to the manager for five years, proposed that he become personnel manager of the bank.

This, of course, was an area of responsibility where Jose could show good evidence of past achievements. His boss was receptive to the proposal. He actually responded by saying, "It's a great solution. I don't know why I didn't come up with it myself."

Each In-company Campaign is unique in the mix between *things you'll have to live with* and *things you can change.* Avoid jumping to emotion-based conclusions in this area. Your observations, together with carefully analyzed feedback from your C/I Network, will enable you to tell the unchangeable factors of your job structure from the changeable ones, and the easily changeable ones from those that are difficult to change. It's always wise to start at the easy end.

Kenneth M., for example, knew that it would be very difficult to get a raise at the hospital he worked in. The salary structure was quite rigid, and his job in the personnel department was assigned a specific grade level. What he could more easily change was the range and nature of his responsibilities. Kenneth proposed to his superior, the personnel director, that the responsibility for equal employment opportunity management be added to Kenneth's current job as employee relations counselor. This new area of responsibility was mostly administrative and could be easily incorporated into Kenneth's work load. Up to now it had been done by a part-time administrator who was leaving the hospital.

Kenneth succeeded with his first In-company Campaign goal and found that he was able to get a grade change for his job. This made it possible to achieve the raise.

Because the emotions have no sense of relative weight, one or two anticipated obstacles in an In-company Campaign can make the task ahead seem huge and unmanageable. In fact, looking at any project as a single huge effort is, emotionally, too taxing for most of us. Don't look at an In-company Campaign as a single project but a *step-by-step process*. Until the very last step is taken, the criterion of measurement is "progress" rather than "success." Any time an obstacle seems mountainous from an emotional point of view, take the rational approach to cut each obstacle into bite-size portions and deal with them one by one. However, on the emotional side, confidence in your objective, and your ability to achieve it, will do more than any amount of skillful argument in convincing your employer. The following story illustrates this point:

> A private vocational counseling firm in the Midwest employed two counselors of opposite temperament. One, a typical extrovert, communicated all his achievements as they happened. Everybody on the premises knew that he was successful with his clients. He received many testimonial letters that he displayed on the walls of his office. The other counselor was a quiet man, equally competent. But no one knew what he was accomplishing; his clients went away after they had been helped, presumably happy, and were never heard from again. By contrast with the other counselor, he looked totally unproductive.
>
> The president of the firm, after two years of non-communication, decided to replace the second counselor with someone more suitable to the image the president wanted to build in the community. The counselor anticipated the event with a preemptive strike: He asked for an increase in salary. The president's stunned reaction was: "He's asking for an increase—we may have been wrong about him." The result was a delay in the dismissal of the counselor.
>
> The counselor had now bought enough time to document his competence and his success with his clients.

He remained on the job and even received the increase requested. Since then he has devoted more time to communicating his achievements to his employer.

This story shows that the implementation of an In-company Campaign is a demonstration of self-confidence and has a positive effect on others. Asking to be rewarded for your work implies that you believe in it. Asking for an opportunity to contribute and to take on more responsibility shows that you believe in your employer. The positive emotional energy generated by your action will carry you over most of the rough spots in an In-company Campaign. Analysis of seeming obstacles and careful next-step planning will help you solve the remaining problems.

A well-planned In-company Campaign proceeds like the proverbial Swiss watch from beginning to successful conclusion. However, in order to help you avoid problems, or to identify and solve them if they do arise, here is a brief review of all four stages of the In-company Campaign, from a problem-eliminating point of view:

Stage	Problem	Prevention/ Solution
I. Setting your objective	Self-serving objective	Look for a balance between benefits to you and benefits to your employer.
	Unrealistic objective	Reality-test your objective using both your research information and your C/I Network. Rewrite your objective.

Stage	Problem	Prevention/Solution
	Complex objective	Consider tackling your objective in two or more steps.
	Vague or very general language	Use only concise language. If you can't focus your objective, it may mean you are not ready for an In-company Campaign. Avoid fishing expeditions hoping for your boss to tell you what your objective should be. Use your C/I Network.
II. Your Written Presentation	Negative, hostile language, implied blame to employer for not being more concerned with your welfare.	Use only positive terms in your first draft. Get feedback from an unbiased third person.
	Long-winded presentation	Respect for your boss's time demands a brief letter, two pages maximum. You can always add more documentation later if needed.

Stage	Problem	Prevention/ Solution
	"Detective Story" format: keeping the reader guessing about your objective until the end	Follow outline in chapter 8. Put objective up front (second paragraph).
III. Making your presentation	"Lukewarm" reception of your presentation	Focus your presentation on: 1. Loyalty to your employer 2. Confidence about your objective, your work, and your ability.
	Objections and obstacles raised	Listen carefully, and propose ways to deal with obstacles. In most cases you won't be able to do this on the spot. Request time to respond. In *no* case volunteer to retreat from your objective or from your In-company Campaign during this meeting.
	A definite response of no	Again, don't give up on the spot. Ask for another discussion. Consider an alternative next step.

Stage	Problem	Prevention/ Solution
IV. Follow-through	No follow-through action on your boss's part, even though promised	Take full responsibility for initiating all follow-through communication.
	Endless discussion but no action	Provide motivation through thank-you notes, positive day-to-day communication, and superior job performance. Think in terms of *some* progress at each discussion.
	Multiple objections brought up by boss one-by-one, or all at once	Consider modifying or changing your objective to make it acceptable to your boss while still retaining benefit to you.
	Revelation of circumstances unknown to you that will permanently prevent you from achieving your objective	Consider leaving the organization in order to find a more favorable job environment.

In our experience the vast majority of the obstacles to job growth and career satisfaction have not been factual or discriminatory, but a misreading of other people's behavior and motivation. After sifting through all the information we have received over the last twenty years, we've found that the *single most devastating obstacle* in the mind of the unhappy employee is expressed by the phrases: "*I know what he'll say*" . . . "I know what she's thinking" . . . "I know why he's doing what he's doing" . . . etc.

Yet thousands of people who have taken positive action to influence and change their work environments have been happily surprised by the realities of their superiors' and associates' actual thought processes and reactions.

You'll find that the rewards of planning and conducting an In-company Campaign—and the positive state of mind it generates—far outweigh any of the minor obstacles along the way.

At the conclusion of this chapter, a philosophical note seems in order: In advocating "working and liking it," we have implied that we are in favor of your "doing your thing." That's true as far as it goes. But none of us exists in a vacuum. Working relationships are reciprocal. An In-company Campaign can only be successful if it benefits you, your associates, and your employers. Every advancement you make at someone else's expense is an illusion. This is a proven fact.

Your work environment is a community, however few or many people are involved. To be successful and happy in your work, you must develop what Richard Bolles calls a "sense of community." So we now move beyond the limits set for this book with this statement: The best way to move ahead is to help someone else to move ahead; the best way to become successful is to help others to be successful; one way to get to like your work is to help others to like their work.

CHAPTER 12

CREATING YOUR
WORK UTOPIA

"Is there a way to get my boss to anticipate my every wish—to come to me and say, 'You are ready for a promotion,' and then offer me the exact new job I want, with the duties I would have chosen for myself?" A reasonable question. The answer is: Of course. Here is a textbook example of just such a case.

A man we know, the owner of a small business, arrived at a point in life where he had serious thoughts of retirement and of finding a successor to take over the business. He was lucky: One of his long-time trusted employees "just happened" to fit the bill perfectly. (We don't think it was luck, but foresight.) On the very day our friend was going to start a conversation with his employee, that man called him on the interoffice phone and said, "Can we have lunch sometime this week? I have something I want to talk over with you." Our friend replied, "Yes, let's do it—there's something I want to discuss with you too."

At lunch they went through a little dance sequence

of "You first!"—"No, *you* first." What had happened, of course, was that both men were so much on the same wavelength through their long-time association that they had the same thought at the same time, and when the dessert and coffee arrived they had concluded an agreement on the method and timing for transferring responsibility for running the business.

This story is not one of a kind. It happens more often than you might think, but rarely out of the blue. In a sense the preceding was a set-up. If you would like to create such a set-up, there's a way to do it, though it takes a little work. It's like creating an on-the-job investment plan. You make relatively small payments and start collecting the return as early as six months later, and for the rest of your career life!

If you've read and understood all the preceding chapters, you are ready to start on your personal investment plan. The easiest way to do this is step-by-step over a period of time. And you will literally win friends and influence people all along the way. The following is an outline of the process of creating your ideal job environment. Take it one step at a time, fully implementing each step, so you'll need very little energy to maintain the momentum while turning your full attention to the next step.

STEP ONE. Get people on your side; set up positive relationships.

The more people are emotionally in tune with you and your actions, the more productive you'll be. So first, align all the human energy in your job environment in your favor. Make a list of all the people with whom you come in daily contact and evaluate their attitudes toward you and your job. Are they on your side? Are they helping you or getting in your way?

We are talking about constructive work relationships, not close personal friendships. Make a plan to win the cooperation of those people on your list with whom you have a neutral or negative relationship, whether they are above you, below you, or on your level from a reporting point of view. See chapter 6 for some ideas on how to do this. Your basic approach will be to take a genuine interest in each of these people, to offer help in an area of your strength, or ask for help in an area of theirs.

You may wonder how others will react to this new initiative of yours. The answer is that if your actions are sincere and constructive, the law of emotional reciprocity will ensure that your advances receive a positive response.

Julian T., for example, worked for a boss he hardly ever saw. Not because of business travel, but because the boss was always in his office with the door shut. Julian was an assistant editor at a large publishing house and depended on his boss for regular assignments, as well as for guidance on what the company expected from its authors.

After months of silence between Julian and his boss, Julian came to the uncomfortable conclusion that he'd never accomplish much unless he started to communicate with his boss.

Julian wasn't sure how it would be received, but he took the first step and said to his boss: "It would be very helpful to me if we could meet regularly to make sure I'm going in the right direction with our authors. Could we meet this afternoon?" Without hesitation, the boss responded: "I think that's a good idea. Let's do it."

Julian was almost shocked and very relieved at the simplicity of starting up positive communications.

The important conclusion we can draw here is this: *Human relations come before productivity!*

It should be obvious that you have a problem if you are still trying to establish human relations six months later and haven't produced anything.

STEP TWO. Set up a long-term process to maintain positive work relationships.

This is done by developing specific positive habits in communicating with others. Consider the following examples:

Alex enters your place of work on a Monday morning, unshaven, hung over, and looking like the cat that's lost its breakfast. He mutters, ". . . lousy weekend . . . both kids in bed with flu . . . have to face this rotten job for another week."

If you're a good friend, you'll be sympathetic the first time it happens, less so the second time, etc. If your relationship is not that close, you may be forgiven for wishing he'd keep his problems to himself. You may even be having problems of your own.

Now Martin arrives at work, smiles as he walks past your desk, and says, "Good morning—have a good weekend?" For all you know his kids are sick too—he may even tell you about it later on—but for a few minutes he made you feel better about Monday mornings.

"Aren't these examples obvious?" you may ask. Let's backtrack for a minute. Remember that the emotions recognize no shades of grey—everything is black and white. In terms of our initial emotional reaction, a smile equals life and a frown equals death. It's only our reasoning ability that makes us see the previous sentence as an exaggeration—an *emotional* exaggeration! Part of our decision-making process starts with instant emotional reactions that can result in major con-

sequences. This is the "reason" decision makers in the
hiring process will offer a job to a person they like,
even in the face of missing qualifications; they almost
never hire anybody they don't like. Afterwards, the
hiring decisions are, of course, validated with impressive logic.

A fact of life in every organization is that, everything else being equal, the person who is perceived as
having his or her emotions under control is considered
reliable, will be given responsibilities, and will ultimately be chosen for leadership roles or any other
roles of his choice. The person who is perceived as being emotionally out of control, on the other hand, will
be quietly passed over. No one voluntarily gets in the
way, or for that matter anywhere near, a vehicle out of
control. A person who gives the impression of being
buffeted by his or her moods, feelings, or circumstances in life does not inspire confidence. At the
feeling level, small daily actions, reactions, and interactions on the job set the emotional climate for far-
reaching events as the job develops. We have seen
abundant evidence that a small cause like a good-
morning smile is ridiculously out of proportion to the
effect it really has.

We must pause here to discuss briefly the meaning
of "emotional control." The myth that self-control is
synonomous with bottled-up feelings and leads to
heart attacks is just that—a myth. The difference between "holding in" and "channeling" is illustrated by
Jeanne W.:

Responsible for all advertising in a major travel agency, Jeanne had designed an innovative ad campaign for
a series of package tours. She was only waiting for the
approval of the firm's president to implement the campaign and see the results pour in. The approval was

slow in coming. The president didn't see the promised bonanza Jeanne envisioned.

Every day that passed added to the pressure build-up in Jeanne's emotions. She started to have night-mares in which she saw the president having dark designs on her sanity and the firm's solvency. After six weeks of this pressure, Jeanne needed relief.

She wrote a letter of resignation. Twenty-four hours later it ended up in her wastebasket. Jeanne had come to a different conclusion: The advertising campaign *was* good and made sense. It was worth a last-ditch ef-fort.

After another check on the cost of the campaign and the expected benefits, she wrote a well-reasoned letter to the president, asking for the opportunity to present her case in person, promising not to mention it any-more if she couldn't convince him. When she met with him, all the negative emotional force she had built up over the past weeks turned into positive energy, and she made an impassioned presentation of her idea. The president was totally convinced.

The interesting part of this story is that, according to Jeanne, the relief from pouring out all this emotional energy would have been equally great even if she hadn't made the sale.

Part of implementing good human relations habits, then, is to learn to channel your emotions. Make sure others see only what you want them to see. In some cases it may be good to show a deliberate measure of anger or disappointment; it's almost always productive to let others see when you feel good (unless you're in a poker game!).

As with any habit you are trying to form, you have to start with *specific* actions. But unlike dieting, you needn't have a sense of deprivation. You are not asked to hold back anything, just convert it into positive en-ergy, positive action, positive communication.

STEP THREE. Build a foundation for producing results.

The timing in this step depends on the kind of work you do. While a customer service representative may need to deal with immediate problems continuously, a nuclear power plant salesperson may not show tangible results so regularly. Both, however, can start building the foundation for their results in an active manner.

We are not suggesting that you become Superman or Wonder Woman immediately following your decision to create a new job environment for yourself. But you have now set good human relations practices in motion and can turn your attention to showing your associates and superiors that you can get things done.

In order to demonstrate your productivity, it's useful to define your job as a series of projects. To illustrate what we mean by this, let's take a relatively simple activity like filing papers.

Barbara van E., the executive secretary and assistant to the president of a hotel corporation, was responsible, among other things, for the maintenance of a filing system she had inherited from a predecessor. It was one of Barbara's minor duties and the files had been maintained reasonably well, but she felt she would be more comfortable with a new system she had set up herself. She proposed to the president that she take three days, while he was going to be away on a short business trip, to review and partially reorganize the file system. Out of enlightened self-interest, the president agreed, and Barbara went ahead with the job. She finished it in two and a half days and demonstrated to the president how well it worked by retrieving a few documents he had had difficulty finding in the past.

This example demonstrates a number of significant points:

1. Barbara chose a good time for the project and checked it with her superior.
2. She told the president what she was going to do, did it, and told him what she had done. She even demonstrated the quality of her work to him.
3. Barbara set a reasonable time frame for the project and completed it ahead of schedule. (She might have promised to do it in a couple of hours, then irritated her boss by still being at it two days later.)

As a fringe benefit, Barbara heard a few days later that the president had told others what an efficient secretary she was, thereby not only paying an unsolicited compliment to Barbara, but also retroactively validating his own good judgment for having chosen Barbara as a secretary in the first place. This is an important part of the rapport-building process.

The reason for redefining your job as a series of projects to be completed is that your superiors must see the connection between cause and effect to have any way to measure and appreciate your productivity, and to reward it. Anyone who knows horses knows that they have considerably shorter memories than people. A horse must be rewarded, with sugar or carrots, etc., within a very short period of time after a special effort, or it won't be aware of the connection. This isn't intended to be unflattering to people—but, at a more intelligent level, the simile holds true for all of us.

In the example of Barbara van E., the project was self-generated and self-assigned. Defining your work in terms of projects is just as important and necessary if your work is assigned by others, as is illustrated by the story of Donald R., sales representative for a large computer firm.

> Don was reassigned to a new territory and was given certain sales objectives for the first year in the new job. Because the firm specialized in large complex systems, the expectations were for few sales but high revenue from each sale. It would not have been reasonable for Don to be out of touch with his superiors for four to six months, when the first sales were expected. So Don prepared a plan of action, similar to a political election campaign plan, specifying how many calls he planned to make and the types of potential customers he planned to contact. He also divided his "campaign" into several phases, including second and third follow-up calls to the same people, and a strategy to get to senior decision makers as quickly as possible.
>
> Two things happened: Don earned a reputation as an effective salesman *before* he made his first sale—normally hard to do. He also made his first sale sooner than expected—due to the good planning of his campaign—thereby anticipating and exceeding the sales objectives he had been given.

If a task you have been given appears huge and complex to you, divide it into smaller portions. Make sure you announce or check out each portion before you start, and communicate successful conclusions as you go along. If your task or job is not well defined or no objectives have been given to you, define your own job and set your own objectives, but never in a vacuum. *Always* get your superiors' agreement beforehand, thereby assuring yourself of their acknowledgment and appreciation afterwards.

STEP FOUR. Find the best method of communicating plans, progress, and results to your boss.

This may seem like a small step, but many people have put necessary roadblocks in their way by ignoring it. Consider these two approaches:

Frank knocks on his boss's door, enters, and says, "I want to tell you what I'm going to do today, just so you know." The boss looks up from his work, glasses halfway down his nose, glares at Frank, and says, "Okay, but can't we talk about it later?"

Frank responds: "It'll only take a minute. Besides, I wouldn't start until I have your approval." He then proceeds for the next twenty minutes to lay out his plans in detail. The boss, not wanting to shatter the new relationship, bites his tongue and says, "Thanks for telling me!" Halfway to the door, Frank turns around and reopens the conversation in a conspiratorial tone: "You know the salesman who's been hanging around outside your office? I've just successfully completed a project of getting rid of him. Let me tell you how I did it." He sits down and proceeds while his boss's feelings first sink and then turn into hostility.

Now look at how Bob handles this situation:

He waits until he sees that his boss isn't heavily involved in a project. Bob then says, "I know you're busy—when you have a few minutes I'd like to talk to you about my next project. Or, if it's more convenient for you, I'll jot it down on a piece of paper and leave it on your desk."

After the project is completed, Bob once again waits for the right moment and, without interrupting his boss, says, "By the way, I finished the project we talked about the other day. When you have a chance, I'd like to talk to you about it."

In this example the boss is being given a choice about both time and manner of communication.

Whenever a complex or relatively long-term project is involved, the plan of action and the result have to be communicated in writing as well as verbally.

These examples are somewhat oversimplified, but the first step is always to find the right time to communicate plans and results and then to find the method best suited to the people and circumstances involved. The preferences of superiors range from short, informal discussions to lengthy, detailed, formal memoranda.

Developing this kind of sensitivity doesn't take long, but it takes your entire attention until it's done. After two or three weeks you should have a good feel for how and when your communication with your superiors works best. Then it will be more or less automatic.

STEP FIVE. Start a log of your achievements.

For the purpose of this plan of action, the words achievement and contribution are synonymous. Any personal achievement that does not represent a contribution to your employer is irrelevant in this context. On the other hand, any contribution, however small, is an achievement.

Anne K., office manager for a real estate management firm, felt that employee morale would be considerably improved by more social interaction. She planned office parties and lunches for every employee occasion—from birthdays to baby showers.

Although Anne considered this an achievement, it actually harmed the firm by taking employees away from their jobs—clearly not a contribution to her employer.

On the other hand, Anne had actually made an important contribution by the manner in which she handled complaint calls from the tenants of several large commercial buildings which her firm managed. Anne's courteous, professional, and quick responses were cited by the property owners as a major attraction for doing more business with her firm. Although responding courteously seemed second nature to Anne, and something "anyone would do," this was undoubtedly an important contribution to her firm.

There are two reasons for keeping a written record of your contributions: It creates a habit of thinking in terms of "contributing," giving you a feeling of being a valid and valuable part of the organization; and it gives you tangible evidence to support a request for recognition and reward when the time is right.

The process of listing contributions is a simple one. Just use a notebook that you keep at work and jot down contributions as you make them before you leave work at night, or before you start in the morning. Don't evaluate the magnitude or value of any entry in your notebook—just collect entries.

Most people who keep a log of their contributions find that they contribute something, large or small, every day. Once you develop this profitable habit, you will at least *not* be in the position of one woman we know who was interviewed for a promotion to head a hospital's personnel department. She was so used to thinking in terms of job descriptions that it had not occurred to her to think any other way. When she was interviewed by a senior administrator, she was asked to describe her contributions in her previous job. She proceeded to list her former duties. The administrator interrupted her and said, "Yes, we know all the things you were responsible for—what we want to know is how well you carried out your responsibilities." The woman was nonplussed. "That's not for me to say, surely," she replied.

This is still a common reaction in the more structured professions. However, there is a growing awareness of the need to think in qualitative terms in the work world. A fringe benefit of becoming aware of your own achievements and contributions is the greater awareness of the contributions of others, and the ability to motivate others by recognizing their contributions.

> *STEP SIX.* Start building your personal Contact/Information Network

Now take stock of what you know about your company or organization. Review the informal organizational diagram you developed. The names and titles of the people you know, and their reporting relationship to each other, also tells you what information you *don't* have, and need to acquire. The next step is to make a list of the people with whom you have an informal talking relationship. Start with the list of immediate associates you made during Step One.

From your organizational diagram, transfer the names of people in key positions whom you should get to know. These people will give you access to information about the organization, its purposes, plans, and problems at any given point in time. Now, cross off your list of current and potential contacts, the names of any people who are known as undependable and unsuccessful in their work. The information you would get from such people would be unreliable and could give you a distorted picture of what is really happening.

> *STEP SEVEN.* Fine-tune your job. Adjust your job description to the reality of your work environment.

Job descriptions have a way of drifting off course almost unnoticed as time slips by. (Also called JDC or Job Description Creep.) Even a month after it was first given to you, your job description will probably have already taken on a life of its own. Whether you started with a vaguely or a very tightly defined job description, you'll find yourself doing something different after a month. (You might also be doing something different from what your boss was expecting.) This is due, in part, to the fact that it's difficult to envision in detail what a particular job, done by a particular person, will really look like in the future. It's also due, in part, to the fact that needs and conditions change slightly in every job from one month to the next.

In truth, there is no point in defining a job within an inch of its life at any time. It's important, however, to take a close look from time to time and adjust your job to the realities of the organization's current conditions and purpose. If left to themselves, job descriptions tend to harden and become more difficult to adjust. To prevent finding yourself in a straitjacket and out of step with your real personality and your employer's purposes, make your adjustment at least once a year, but preferably every six months.

If you wait too long, you may be in the position of a cargo ship that set out from England on a course for Argentina. It would be a disaster for that ship to make its first course correction when it found itself off Cape Hatteras. By the time the ship finally arrived in Buenos Aires, the owners have probably collected the insurance money and written off the cargo. Don't get written off by your employer!

Start by either discussing your job with your boss, or write down your job description as you see it and then ask your boss to comment on it. Remember you can only do a good job if *you* are comfortable with your job description. So keep both your employer and yourself happy.

The timing of discussing your job with your boss is, of course, an important consideration. As long as you choose a time when he or she is reasonably free of pressure, and your relationship is in a positive mode, your sincere desire to clarify your understanding of your employer's expectations will never be rebuffed.

The following is an example of what can happen to job descriptions:

> Albert K. took up his new job as quality-control manager in a light bulb manufacturing plant. His job was to keep the reject rate of mass-produced light bulbs down to a minimum. One of the traditional techniques he employed was, periodically, to drop light bulbs on the floor from a certain height to see how many survived. Albert soon tired of his job, which involved a lot of record keeping and statistical analysis, besides the obvious peril of walking on broken glass.
>
> From an "after-the-fact" quality-control job, his activities gradually, over a period of a few weeks, drifted to before-the-fact quality assurance. He now spent most of his time experimenting with different design ideas, glass mixtures, and temperature cycles. Not only was Albert not qualified to work in this area, but he produced no tangible improvements, and the person hired for that job, a trained specialist, resented Albert's amateur interference.
>
> Meanwhile the reject and return rate of light bulbs went up through inattention. Albert retrieved the situation barely in time to survive in the job. Next, he made peace with the specialist and worked out an agreement for future collaboration that gave him some involvement in design improvements, making his job more interesting.

If this course correction had not been made, three things would have happened: One, he would have caused a permanent split between two functions that normally need a cooperative effort; two, he would have been depressed by lack of progress and failure in a discipline in which he had no training; and three, Albert would probably have been fired for neglecting his main duty, quality control.

STEP EIGHT. Set long-range goals.

All of us need to feel we are making progress. But in the absence of a goal, it's very difficult to measure progress. What does it benefit us to become better at something in which we don't have any interest in the first place, or to proceed further toward a destination at which we don't ultimately want to arrive? Make sure you have meaningful goals.

To help you in the goal-setting process, here's a simple technique you can use as a starting point: State on paper where you want to be in your job a year from now. (If your employer asks you to engage in this kind of goal setting, as some now do, you'll be in good shape by starting the process on your own.) Describe in detail how you see your skills, your job description, and your relationships with people at the end of the first year. Create a picture, using your imagination, to fill in the parts about which you don't have much factual information. For instance, you may have to guess the speed with which you can acquire certain skills, how you'll like using those skills, the amount of help you'll get from others, your company's financial position at that time, and your life situation.

It's useful to pause here and discuss briefly the role played by the imagination in work. It's becoming increasingly evident that the left side of the brain favors numbers, facts, data, analysis, and structure, while the right side favors intuition, imagination, synthesis, and risk taking. Richard Bolles, author and career-development pioneer, has written about the uses you can make of this knowledge. To paraphrase Bolles, when we run out of data, we can engage our intuitive and imaginative faculties. In fact, we limit ourselves unnecessarily whenever we rely entirely on the left side of our brain, even though that appears to be the side automatically favored by most people.

It's perfectly reasonable to include both factual and intuitive data in your projection of where you are going to be a year from now. What we are proposing is that you paint an *ideal* picture of your work situation then. There is always time to scale it down to "realistic" proportions, but the first task is to set the best and highest goal possible. You will adjust this ideal picture by filling in facts and data as they become known to you. Your goal must be one you can almost "taste," to make any progress toward it worthwhile. The set time of one year is, of course, arbitrary. You may just as easily set a two-year or a five-year goal. Any goal can be corrected, adjusted, or changed, but having no goal is unacceptable. Here is an example of one of the infinite variety of such personal goals:

Graham B., a young research scientist, had been assigned, at his own request, to an R&D project involving laser materials. Graham soon became aware that the project was poorly managed and that the talents of the staff were not used to anything near their full capacity.

Having recently discovered in himself an interest in what motivates people to effective teamwork, he decided to set a personal goal of heading up a project team similar to the one to which he had just been assigned. Graham began by finding out the technical requirements for project management. Then he made a one-year plan for achieving his goal of being given total responsibility for his own project.

Graham's plan consisted of a number of theoretical and practical steps including updating his knowledge of crystallography as well as staffing and managing a project. The plan also included the necessary step of convincing his superiors that he was capable of handling the responsibility involved in managing a complex project. To complete his plan, Graham studied all the project reports he could get his hands on. This gave him a good theoretical knowledge of project communications, and their importance in project leadership.

By midyear Graham expected to be responsible for a small group of technicians, thereby proving that he could get people to work together and produce results.

In Graham's mind there was now a complete picture of what he wanted to achieve in a year's time, and the milestones he'd have to pass on the way to that goal. He was aware that there might be unforeseen obstacles. He also hoped for some shortcuts and lucky breaks on the way. All in all, he was confident that he had a good chance to reach his goal.

A factor common to all goals is personal growth or self-education. Education doesn't stop with graduation from school or college. It continues in both formal and informal ways. Make sure that continued learning or study is amply represented in your ideal goal.

STEP NINE. Implement your long-range goals.

A goal requires a plan of action as a bridge from where you are to where you are going. Without it the goal becomes a daily reminder of failure. The more specific your goal is, the easier it is to form a plan of action. If, for example, you are in charge of a group of people, and part of your twelve-month goal is to have a 100 percent productive department, you know that you have to help a few unproductive employees to become productive, or replace them by the end of that time.

An important factor in this process is how others perceive you. Get your associates and superiors used to your forward movement. Provided they benefit by your progress, they'll get into the spirit of the thing and help you move.

We recently talked to the president of a manufacturing company. He described the sequence of events that led him to appoint one of his divisional production managers to the position of vice-president in charge of operations for the entire company. These are the company president's words:

"When I first met him, he was full of plans for his own future in his job. Even though his plans made sense, I thought that maybe he was just full of hot air. I was even worried that he'd make waves and sidetrack others.

"After a while I began to accept his attitude as normal for him. I even noticed that he had a good effect on others by being positive about the company and about himself.

"One day I realized that the production figures in his division had increased significantly over those of the other divisions. I said to myself, Hey—this guy is *good!*

"My final move was to call him into my office to talk to him about a bigger job. I think if I had waited, he would have come to my office not more than twenty-four hours later to ask for the job."

STEP TEN. Bring your home life in tune with your work life.

Create a balance between *all* aspects of your life. Any discrepancy will eat up energy and seriously hurt your relationships with others at work and at home.

Pauline D., for example, was promoted to regional director of operations in a multibranch food service chain. To get her new job under control, she packed a bag, got on an airplane, and started a life that alternated between hotel rooms, airports, local food service outlets, and more airplanes.

She had left three teenage children and a husband behind for whom the pride in Pauline's career advancement was hollow compensation for her physical absence. After three weeks of this, they managed to get their message across to Pauline in a few evening phone calls. The net effect of these conversations on Pauline was loss of several nights sleep, increased guilt feelings, and a certain abruptness in her communications with the local managers whom she had come to visit.

Pauline packed her bag again and went home to take stock of the situation. With some help, she realized that there was another, more effective way to do her new job. By developing a tight communications system that included daily written and telephone reports from the local managers in her region, Pauline found that occasional short trips (never on Sundays!) kept her completely in touch with all the key people. The operation functioned better than it had when she was traveling and occasionally lost sight of one part of her territory while concentrating on another.

Very often even small changes in something like working hours, for people whose hours are flexible, can play a major role in adjusting the balance between different aspects of the work/life continuum.

Another area of possible adjustment is talent utilization. Not all your talents may be used in your job. If, for instance, your creative faculty or your physical energy is not in demand in your job, create a balance by creative or physical activity during your nonwork hours. It has long been known that a talent or skill not used turns back on its owner and becomes a source of frustration.

Doris V., chief acountant for a chain of retail stores, serves as a typical example. Her unusual talent for observing and recalling facts and details of every event of which she was a part, while being very useful in her profession, turned against her when it came to events outside of the store. Working long hours and having a limited social life, she had few friends and acquaintances with whom to share her observations.

Doris was also a compulsive raconteur, which led her to treat her associates at work to detailed accounts of every movie and television program she had seen and every social function in which she had ever even been slightly involved. She soon found that people began to avoid her, or made excuses to cut her narrative short. This, in turn, caused Doris to be hostile towards others.

The problem was solved almost accidentally. Doris had a friend who wrote reviews of social and artistic events for the major local newspaper. This friend asked Doris if she would be willing to try her hand at attending and reviewing two upcoming weekend events while he had to be out of town unexpectedly. Doris jumped at the opportunity and, to no one's surprise, turned out interesting, detailed, and sparkling accounts of both events. With the paper's permission, Doris and her friend divided the review column between them with Doris reviewing some evening and all weekend events. Having found another creative outlet for her talents, her relationship with her associates at work improved within weeks.

To help you create your ideal job environment, your personal career utopia, here are the ten steps in summary:

Step One. Set up positive relationships with your co-workers

Step Two. Develop communications habits to maintain positive relationships

Step Three. Develop a reputation for producing tangible results

Step Four.   Set up systems for communicating results as well as plans and progress to your superiors

Step Five.   Start a log of your achievements and contributions

Step Six.   Build your own C/I Network

Step Seven. Review, correct, and fine-tune your job description

Step Eight. Set up long-range goals

Step Nine.   Implement your long-range goals

Step Ten.   Create a balance between your work and other parts of your life.

The last step is perhaps the most important. Without it, steps one through nine may have only limited usefulness. Our work has convinced us that ultimate fulfillment in one's job, one's career, and one's life depends on a *balance* between a variety of elements.

We've given many examples of this: Direct verbal communication between people is supported and balanced by a powerful written presentation; the emotions are balanced and made acceptable by reason; and reason is fueled by emotions. Imagination and intuition of the right side of the brain are balanced by structure and the capacity for facts and figures of the left side of the brain. Benefit to self is equivalent to, and dependent on, benefit to others. Finally, work itself must be balanced by recreation and by avocation.

To bring these various elements into perfect tune with each other takes a lifetime for most of us. Every step in the process is worthwhile and brings tangible rewards. And there is always another step. What's *your* next step?

ABOUT THE AUTHORS

RICHARD GERMANN is an international career management consultant with over eighteen years of experience in his field. In his position as Director of Client Services for the national career counseling firm of Bernard Haldane Associates, Mr. Germann was responsible for the organization's total counseling program, its content, quality, and continual improvement. Mr. Germann is the principal author of *Job and Career Building*, and is currently a Director of Lander Corporate Services, a human resources and career management consulting firm in Britain. Mr. Germann has also been a contributing columnist with the *Boston Herald* and continues to make radio and television appearances to advise the public on job and career issues. Currently he is a principal of Richardson, Reid & Associates, a Boston-based career management and human resources consulting firm. He resides in Boston with his wife, Sheridan.

DIANE BLUMENSON is a career management consultant, writer, and frequent television and radio guest. She currently appears regularly on WLVI-TV in Boston, contributing her "Working" feature on the New England *Today* show. Ms. Blumenson has been a contributing columnist for the *Boston Herald American* and *Working Woman* magazine, and was the writer and coproducer of a job and career information series for WEEI radio in Boston. Ms. Blumenson has a strong background in public relations and spent seven years as Director of Public Information and career counselor with the national firm, Bernard Haldane Associates. Most recently she founded the consulting firm of Richardson, Reid & Associates. She lives in Westwood, Massachusetts with her husband and two children.

PETER ARNOLD is a communications consultant and writer. He heads a Boston-area firm, Peter Arnold Associates, that provides communications, corporate public relations, and writing services to New England and New York clients. Mr. Arnold has authored or coauthored ten nonfiction books, including *Job and Career Building* with Richard Germann and *The Job Search* Companion with Ellen J. Wallach. He lives near Boston with his wife, Margery, and stepson, Derek.